OYSTER PERPETUAL DATEJUST 41

SEIZE THE DAY... TOMORROW.

Casper | CASPER.COM/KINFOLK

LAMBERT & FILS
studio

Made in Montréal

Lars Gitz Architects

HeartOak. The essence of nature.

Unique wooden floors since 1898.

dinesen.com

Creativity is allowing yourself to make mistakes. Art is knowing which ones to keep.

— Scott Adams

SØRENSEN

Sorensen. Luxury leather for the most
iconic designs in the world

PEAU SØRENSEN LEATHER
S
LEDER PIEL
19 73
LÆDER

Frame: MYKITA DECADES SUN BUENO | Photography: Mark Borthwick

MYKITA

BERLIN | CARTAGENA | COPENHAGEN | LOS ANGELES | MONTERREY
NEW YORK | PARIS | TOKYO | VIENNA | WASHINGTON | ZERMATT | ZURICH

SHOP ONLINE AT MYKITA.COM

PREMIUM SUBSCRIPTION

Enjoy four issues per year, plus full access to Kinfolk.com, a set
of notecards and 10% off your next online purchase.

i iittala

Ruutu
Design by Ronan and
Erwan Bouroullec

iittala.com/ruutu

KINFOLK

EDITOR-IN-CHIEF
Nathan Williams

EDITOR
Julie Cirelli

CREATIVE DIRECTOR
Anja Charbonneau

DEPUTY EDITOR
John Clifford Burns

DESIGN DIRECTOR
Alex Hunting

ASSISTANT EDITOR
Molly Mandell

COPY EDITOR
Rachel Holzman

CASTING DIRECTOR
Sarah Bunter

MANAGING DIRECTOR
Doug Bischoff

COMMUNICATIONS DIRECTOR
Jessica Gray

ADVERTISING DIRECTOR
Pamela Mullinger

PUBLISHING DIRECTOR
Amy Woodroffe

**SALES & DISTRIBUTION
DIRECTOR**
Frédéric Mähl

WEB EDITOR
Nikolaj Hansson

ACCOUNTING MANAGER
Paige Bischoff

OUUR DESIGNER
Mario Depicolzuane

STUDIO MANAGER
Monique Schröder

OUUR COLLECTION DESIGNER
Hanna Rauhala

EDITORIAL ASSISTANTS
Lucy Ballantyne
Charlotte Long

DESIGN ASSISTANTS
Benja Pavlin
Federico Sher
Anne Texier
Océane Torti

CONTRIBUTING EDITORS
Michael Anastassiades
Jonas Bjerre-Poulsen
Ilse Crawford
Frida Escobedo
Margot Henderson
Leonard Koren
Amy Sall
Hans Ulrich Obrist
Matt Willey

ILLUSTRATION
Chidy Wayne

**STYLING, PRODUCTION
& SET DESIGN**
Kyle Bean
Marisa Competello
Rose Forde
James Gear
Lucy-Ruth Hathaway
Debbie Hsieh
Sam Jaspersohn
Charlotte Long
Brooke McClelland

SALES & E-COMMERCE ASSISTANT
Martine Christiansen

OUUR COLLECTION ASSISTANT
Stephanie Zingg

WORDS
Alex Anderson
Lucy Ballantyne
Harriet Fitch Little
Charmaine Li
Jessica Lynne
Sean Michaels
Emily Nathan
David Plaisant
Asher Ross
Charles Shafaieh
Suzanne Snider
Rebecca Solnit
Pip Usher
Molly Young

PHOTOGRAPHY
Alisa Aiv
Rune Buch
Elliott Erwitt
David Farrell
Christopher Ferguson
Romain Laprade
Jacques Henri Lartigue
Charlotte Long
Godfrey MacDomnic
Irving Penn
Mads Perch
Guy Le Querrec
Brian Seed
Matthew Sprout
Nina Subin
Marsý Hild Þórsdóttir
Aaron Tilley
Zoltan Tombor
Pia Winther
Alexander Wolfe

ISSUE 24

info@kinfolk.com
www.kinfolk.com

Published by Ouur Media
Amagertorv 14, Level 1
1160 Copenhagen, Denmark

The views expressed in Kinfolk magazine are those of the respective contributors and are not necessarily shared by the company or its staff.

SUBSCRIBE
Kinfolk is published four times a year. To subscribe, visit kinfolk.com/subscribe or email us at info@kinfolk.com

CONTACT US
If you have questions or comments, please write to us at info@kinfolk.com. For advertising inquiries, get in touch at advertising@kinfolk.com

Publication Design
by Alex Hunting

Printed in Canada
by Hemlock Printers Ltd.

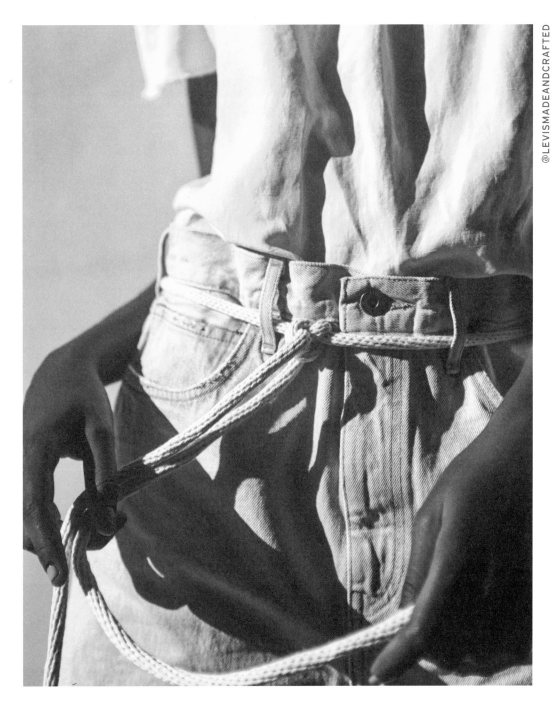

LEVI'S®
MADE & CRAFTED®

ARTFUL CONSTRUCTION. ELEVATED DETAILS.
LEVI'S® BY DESIGN.

"For all my attempts to not fit in, I really do belong to my community."
JUNOT DÍAZ – P. 185

The all new PLAYBASE

It really ties the room together.

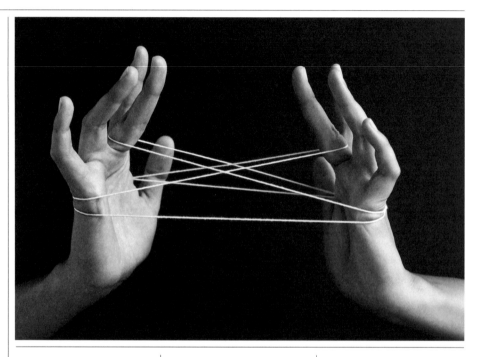
"*Controlling the past begins by knowing it; the stories we tell about who we were and what we did shape what we can do.*"
REBECCA SOLNIT — P.75

Photograph: Zoltan Tombor

COMPASS

Guiding you home.

From this airy Manhattan townhouse to modern
Los Angeles lofts, discover America's finest real estate
and the best agents to guide you there.

compass.com

WHiT

whit-ny.com

Welcome

"I encounter millions of bodies in my life; of these millions, I may desire some hundreds; but of these hundreds, I love only one." *A Lover's Discourse* was French theorist Roland Barthes' treatise on the semiotics of love and attraction, his attempt to untangle the web of love, desire and partnership. By examining the vocabulary we use to make sense of love— words like "tenderness," "languor," "silence" and "jealousy"—Barthes charted a language fraught with passion and risk. Of the word "adorable," he wrote: "Herein a great enigma, to which I shall never possess the key. Why is it that I desire so-and-so? Why is it that I desire so-and-so lastingly, longingly?"

We examine questions like these in this issue's special section on relationships. What are the qualities that draw and bind us? And what kind of emotional scaffolding is required to support those relationships: to mine the raptures of intimacy or the deep veins of trust and loyalty; to overcome the internal fight against self-doubt or the struggle to accept oneself in the face of another? For Isabel and Ruben Toledo, a lifetime of reciprocal creativity has served as a powerful philter, drawing them together in the face of hardship. For psychologist Stephen Trudeau, good congress is found in the balance between independence and attachment. For tantric expert Barbara Carrellas, it is in the trust-building potential of sexual intimacy.

Elsewhere in the issue, we recreate iconic works of art using breakfast foods, from Dalí's melting clock reimagined in fried eggs to Alexander Calder's mobiles restrung with pancakes and syrup. On page 74, Rebecca Solnit argues for the urgency of remaining hopeful—and having a long memory—in times of political upheaval, and on page 184, Pulitzer-winning novelist Junot Díaz discusses the feelings of alienation that drive his semi-autobiographical fiction. Asher Ross explores the role of inner monologue in fomenting personal identity, while Harriet Fitch Little examines the power of silence as a means of communicating resistance, calmness and strength. Silence has the power to elevate conversation above platitudes, she writes, though its mastery is granted to few. "Sometimes, silence speaks volumes."

JULIE CIRELLI

SUMMER 2017

1

Starters

Inside Voices

How and why we talk to ourselves.

Let's do an experiment. Try to remember what was going through your mind right before you began reading. Concentrate on whether your thoughts had the quality of spoken words. If so, what were they saying? Were they dithering over a work email? Shouting out a preference for dinner? I've made it difficult for you, of course, because now you've had to summon a new voice in order to read. But before you began reading, there might have been another voice coursing freely through your mind.

Inner speech seems to be an essential part of our experience. It pays court to our memories, deciphering our conscience and our desires. It murmurs and chants in the most elemental corridors of our minds. It may be rooted in the avid listening we did as children, an internalization of the conversations we heard everywhere around us. It is both social and deeply personal. No one else can hear it but you.

Human beings exhibit an astounding variety of inner speech. Yours might often be simple and practical ("Don't forget the carrots!"), while for others it might expand into a complex and subtle monologue. Think of Virginia Woolf's free-associating protagonist Mrs. Dalloway on her very first page; so happy to be buying the flowers herself, so worried about her past, integrating memory and hope, fear and delight in one seamless interior voice. Perhaps your inner speech comes in a very condensed form—words that could fill pages and pages but which transpire in the flash of a moment.

The vast phenomenology of voice-hearing and inner speech is the specialty of psychologist and author Charles Fernyhough. His book *The Voices Within* begins with a thought-experiment like the one offered above and continues on a wide-ranging yet intimate tour of the subject. On the historical front, Fernyhough reminds us how essential voice-hearing was for the heroes of the *Iliad*, and the role it played in the profound religious experience of women like Margery Kempe, Julian of Norwich and Joan of Arc. A novelist himself, Fernyhough also investigates the role of inner voices for writers—Philip K. Dick, Charles Dickens, Charlotte Brontë, and yes, Virginia Woolf.

Alongside this cultural history, Professor Fernyhough offers a scientific framework for understanding the many forms interior speech can take. One particularly interesting subject is dialogic inner speech, the kind that presents differing perspectives. "Along with helping us to perform better and manage our emotions," Fernyhough writes, "inner dialogue can open up some distinctively creative ways of thinking, in which we can think about what we are doing by taking the critical and constructive perspective of another." Fernyhough suggests that dialogic inner speech plays a key role in allowing us to keep open minds. When engaged in this type of thinking we can propose new thoughts or experiences for consideration and then listen as different voices weigh in. The clues provided by his research seem to show that such thinking activates cooperation between regions in both hemispheres of the brain, including, curiously, an area associated with thinking about other people's minds.

Fernyhough gives ample evidence of inner speech as a core human experience but is careful to note that it's not universal. A minority of test subjects report having no inner speech at all. As for the rest of us, the chatter isn't constant; there are certain times when no inner voice is present. "When I'm playing music—particularly when I'm improvising—the inner dialogue just stops," says Fernyhough by phone from the University of Durham in the UK. "Inner dialogue is probably the main tool of my creativity and productivity, but everybody needs to put the tools down from time to time. And the things I do to rest seem to be the things that help me silence it."

Perhaps most interesting are those rare voices that seem to come from outside. Not the differing attitudes of inner dialogue, nor the unyielding tones of auditory hallucination, but the speech of friends, lovers, foes and family that occasionally materialize in the mind's ear. They arrive unannounced, dispensing advice, sharing words of encouragement, or unearthing a long-avoided thought. These voices walk a peculiar line between memory and fresh thought, and they often bring intense emotions along with them. The poet C.P. Cavafy wrote that they restore "the first poetry of our lives."

Monologue, dialogue, a choir of selves in costume—the sheer variety of inner speech is wonderful and strange. These voices may tax us at times, or keep us awake when we'd rather sleep. Yet to learn about them, to listen carefully, is to glimpse the machinery that creates the self, and perhaps to grow a bit more comfortable within our own minds.

Charles Fernyhough's book *The Voices Within* aims to better understand a realm of the mind that many researchers once thought too subjective and too difficult for scientific observation. Henry James once likened it to "trying to turn up the gas quickly enough to see how the darkness looks."

CHARLES SHAFAIEH

Total Recall

Memory is selective, so why is minutiae so important?

Can anyone become detail oriented or is it an ingrained trait? Popular science and psychology would have us believe the latter. Despite evidence to the contrary, the notion persists that humans are either "left-brained" creative or "right-brained" analytical. We would expect that the latter would be more sensitive to picking up details. Untrue. The theory—like many that characterize personality—is an oversimplification of neural activity: While some functions *are* localized in a particular hemisphere, studies show activity on both sides of the brain during the execution of most tasks, including those that require attention to detail. It's a skill, and like most skills, it can be honed or neglected. So we can, in fact, train our senses to notice subtle details.

Memory plays a crucial role in how we assimilate details. Memory, too, can be strengthened through training, and this training is a prerequisite for learning to pick up on details. One effective way of improving memory, devised in ancient Greece and utilized during the Renaissance, is mastering the mnemonic device known as the "memory palace." Through this method, vast quantities of information are given a visual and spatial dimension that

allows for increased storage and quicker recollection. Why focus on the details, though? The late German philosopher Theodor Adorno insisted on their value to society, particularly concerning music. Rock and pop were abominations to his ear because he believed that, due to what he deemed their musical simplicity, they could be experienced passively and, in turn, lead to a lazy, compliant audience. Conversely, the bracing, atonal compositions of Alban Berg or Beethoven's late work demand the listener's intense engagement. Actively focusing on sonic subtleties, Adorno argued, can prime people to pay attention to other details.

Being finely attuned to detail has both advantages and disadvantages. Those who have the ability also run the risk of developing debilitating obsessions. And while it's a sought-after skill in the workplace, it may blind an employee to the more conceptual levels of problem-solving. In the social realm, it can be challenging for a careful observer to know when to comment or stay silent. These risks notwithstanding, if this trait enables us to slow down and embrace the nuances of our surroundings, we might find that developing it will enrich our lives as well as help us better society.

TINY FURNITURE
by Molly Mandell

Miniature objects have little to offer but their charm. Impossibly small and intricate—and often startlingly expensive—miniatures serve no practical function beyond the feat of their tiny, minutely detailed existence. Yet they remain pleasing objets d'art for professional collectors and dabblers alike, markets to which the Vitra Design Museum has been uniquely attuned. The museum is renowned for its iconic chair collection and offers a trip through seating history, from Michael Thonet to Arne Jacobsen and Ronan and Erwan Bouroullec. For more than two decades Vitra has been producing replicas at exactly one-sixth of the original size so that connoisseurs can curate their own mini home seating displays. Among the models are Marcel Breuer's Wassily Chair (top), designed in 1925, Frank Lloyd Wright's Taliesin West Chair (middle), first produced in 1946, and Grete Jalk's 1963 GJ Bow Chair (bottom).

PIP USHER

Minotaure

Lavish covers and literati contributors: the lasting mystique of a 1930s Parisian periodical.

In 1933, a Swiss publisher by the name of Albert Skira moved to Paris looking to launch an avant-garde periodical. The French capital had just roared through a robustly creative decade (coined *les années folles*, or the crazy years) and emerged as the epicenter of Europe's new artistic scene. Skira, who had already commissioned the talents of Matisse, Picasso and others for his lavish poetry books, now wanted to publish a magazine that championed these contemporary attitudes to a select readership.

Enter André Breton, founder of surrealism and leader of the intellectual fight to prioritize self-expression over convention. In his groundbreaking manifesto on the 20th-century movement, *Manifeste du Surréalisme*, Breton declared that surrealism is "dictated by thought, in the absence of any control exercised by reason, exempt from any aesthetic or moral concern." He and his fellow freethinkers—Man Ray, Salvador Dalí, Marcel Duchamp and others—were famed for their Freudian preoccupation with dreams, the subconscious mind and mental illness.

Breton was to be editor of the new magazine—titled *Minotaure*—alongside fellow surrealist Pierre Mabille. The only rule was that the devoted Marxist had to keep his left-leaning political views out of the magazine's pages in favor of slightly less revolutionary musings on art, literature and technology. In June of 1933, the first issue was published and featured a lavish cover by Picasso depicting the mythological Greek Minotaur—part man, part bull—clutching a dagger in one hand. The message was clear: Surrealism wasn't taking any prisoners.

Over the next six years, 12 additional issues were published. One cover by Spanish painter Joan Miró proved a master class in bold color, its sparse palette of red, white and blue outlining that same mythological creature. Salvador Dalí's cover in 1936 was as eye-catching as one might expect from the erotica-obsessed provocateur: a bull's head, tongue lolling, perched atop a scantily-clad woman's body with a lobster crawling from her midsection. It wasn't the only contribution that Dalí would make to the magazine; his writing also appeared in eight issues.

As war rolled into Europe in 1939, the periodical was halted. France toppled to Hitler's advances and the surrealists scattered—Breton and Dalí emigrated to New York City for several years while Miró returned to Spain's Franco regime. By the time the artists returned, European art had evolved again, now consumed with attempting to understand the mass trauma that the continent had endured. *Minotaure* never resumed publication.

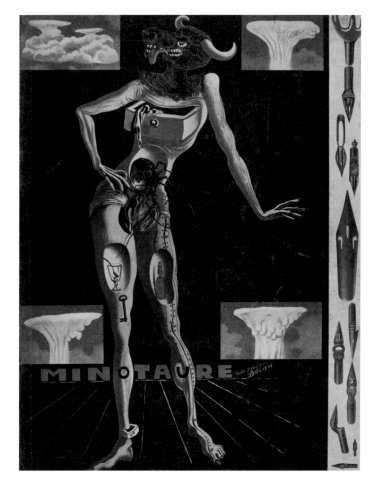

Minotaure's covers included artwork from artists like Diego Rivera, Henri Matisse and Marcel Duchamp. This cover was designed by Salvador Dalí in 1936 for the magazine's eighth issue.

ASHER ROSS

Irving Penn's Corner

An unassuming studio set-up that painted its guests into a corner.

It was perhaps to poke fun at the enigma of fame, and certainly to disrupt it, that photographer Irving Penn would place his most famous subjects in a narrow corner to have their portraits taken. The prop was simple in its contrivance, just two studio flats arranged at a sharply acute angle, but it sufficed to recast his famous subjects in a less complacent light. There they would stay, these celebrated men and women, until they showed us something new.

Many believe that Penn, along with his rival, Richard Avedon, elevated fashion photography to the status of fine art in the public eye. But Penn himself remained worried about the distinction. He threw himself into private work whenever he could—still lifes, anthropological photography (he would haul a portable studio into the field), the famous midsection nudes. Anything to prove that he wasn't limited to the Apollonian perfection of his corporate and magazine work.

The corner portraits strike something of a middle ground, though they aim to capture truth more than beauty. They lack the sharp tonal contrast of Penn's fashion shoots. And instead of maintaining impossibly upright postures, the subjects slouch, lean and loom; they sulk and feign shame. Some crush themselves away from the camera; others seem ready to devour it. For all this, the scenes are framed with Penn's signature formal steadiness.

Penn was a keen witness to the effect his lens had on his subjects, and he liked to say that his corner had a soothing influence. Once soothed, his subjects did the strangest, most arresting things. Marcel Duchamp tried to out-observe the observer; Truman Capote, unbearably vulnerable, wondered whether we might still love him once words had failed. The elderly Georgia O'Keeffe offered the cold humor of a Sicilian grandmother, and the boxer Joe Louis sat deflated and gentle.

If one had to choose a favorite, it might be the shot of Marlene Dietrich. Her insouciant face masks long suffering, which masks insouciance in turn. The greatest eyebrows of all time hover over a rectangular black outfit, behind which her pinned elbows disappear. The hands seem almost disembodied. Stare a while and the dress becomes a kind of void into which the corner recedes endlessly. "You've caught me," she seems to say. "Do come in."

Penn's photographs have memorialized personalities such as Charles James (left) and Elsa Schiaparelli (right)—two fashion designers, who, in the early 20th century, were considered some of the best in their field.

A young entrepreneur on building a sisterhood over social media.

MOLLY MANDELL

Mari Giudicelli

Mari, pictured here wearing a top by Jacquemus, hopes to eventually grow her business to a size that would allow her to donate a percentage of her profits to women's rights organizations.

Brazilian designer Mari Giudicelli was a regular face on New York's fashion circuit long before she launched her eponymous line of women's shoes. As a muse for cult fashion designers Maryam Nassir Zadeh, Eckhaus Latta and Ulla Johnson, she seemed more like a friend who was casually hanging around trying on clothes than a traditional model. The mules and loafers she now designs for her shoe line have the same understated appeal. But behind the scenes, Mari is hardworking, practical and caught perennially in the juggling act of a young entrepreneur.

You manage all aspects of your business, on top of occasionally modeling for other designers. How do you balance everything? Working on all aspects of the business was really valuable when I started out, because it allowed me to build the brand into exactly what I wanted. The first year was an enormous learning curve, but I'm grateful for that. Hiring my first employee will be a milestone, and will take a lot off my shoulders. One of the most important things I've had to learn about achieving balance is knowing when to ask for help.

How have you come to team up with other women in your field? My modeling career definitely helped me connect with some amazing, talented people. New York has a very special group of female designers who have been my role models. It's a competitive city to make something based on beauty, but these women are succeeding in a very solid way. I also reach out to people who I'd like to know better and try not to let my shyness get the best of me. I really want to connect and exchange, and sometimes, the best way to do that is to just say so.

What advice do you have for connecting with a physical community in a digital age? Reach out! Social media makes it so simple to connect with people. If you admire someone's work, don't just "like" it—send a message and tell the person how their work makes you feel. Be honest and respectful, and maybe even invite them to have a cup of coffee with you. You never know what will happen, but in my experience, people tend to respond positively. People want to connect with each other, and it's important to believe in that.

Code of Silence

Don't suffer in silence. Own it.

Silence is not associated with good conversations. In social situations, we value those with the knack to keep on talking, the friends who can parry every awkward pause and slip-up with wit, erudition and a smile. "Conversation should touch everything, but should concentrate itself on nothing," counseled Oscar Wilde—a man who was himself so blessed with the gift of the gab that even his adversaries (and he had many) would admit to being relieved to see him across the table at a dinner party.

But often, in a crowded room, it is not the people talking the loudest who are most in control. In *Pride and Prejudice*, it was Mr. Darcy's appearance of being above the fray of societal tittle-tattle that made him the object of Elizabeth's affections. Almost two centuries later, everywoman heroine Bridget Jones would greet the overlong pauses of her own aloof Mark Darcy with similarly weak knees. The "strong silent type" has proved a resilient romantic lead.

And, while silence has often connoted subordination, some of our most powerful images of resistance in recent years are of people refusing to respond or engage. Think of Ieshia Evans—the Black Lives Matter protester whose image went viral last July when she was pictured facing down Baton Rouge riot police, standing calmly in a sundress, her head raised as if she were looking through, not at, the men trying to remove her from the road. As she told CBS News afterward: "It was just a lot of nonverbal communication. Sometimes, silence speaks volumes."

That not speaking can convey meaning is clear. Cicero—Roman orator and perhaps the world's first etiquette coach—wrote in 44 B.C. that "silence is one of the great arts of conversation," along with taking turns, sticking to subjects of general interest and not

getting grumpy. Ever since, writers have delighted in elaborating on his maxim. The 17th-century memoirist François Duc de La Rochefoucauld identified four types of silence: one that signaled approval, one that conveyed condemnation, one that showed respect and one that indicated discretion. He was writing at a time when such things mattered. From the 17th until the early 20th century, literary salons and coffee houses were Europe's most important intellectual forums, and reputations could be made or undone by conversational aptitude alone. Given the seriousness of the matter, the *duc* cautioned that it would be best for most people to avoid trying to deploy silence in an intentional way: It was a mastery "granted to very few," and even they were prone to mistakes.

The best description of the particular power that staying silent can convey comes from the great German philosopher of language, Martin Heidegger. In his seminal 1927 work, *Being and Time*, he pinpoints silence as the thing that has the power to elevate a conversation above platitudes: "Keeping silent authentically is possible only in genuine discoursing," he wrote. "One's reticence makes something manifest, and does away with 'idle talk'."

Heidegger juggled words in such a way that he was notoriously difficult even for other philosophers to understand. To clarify what "keeping silent authentically" involves, I sought the counsel of a less theoretical commentator: Judy Apps, the British author of *The Art of Conversation*.

On the phone from her home in Surrey, Apps tells me she is in agreement with Heidegger (although she does not frame it as such) that often the most confident people are the ones who are happy to let silences sit for a while.

"People who take their time and are at ease enough to not mind the silence are the most impressive [conversationalists] and often come up with the best answers too," she says.

Her case in point is Barack Obama, whose interviews she studied when writing her book. "You'd hear the question come from the press, and he didn't leap straight in with a formulaic reply. He gave it a little pause and it felt really powerful. It felt like he was really considering the question," she says.

Heidegger shared the Duc de La Rochefoucauld's skepticism that we could "learn" silence: "Non-skilled conversationalists render silence that seemingly signifies their subordination," he cautioned.

Apps is more optimistic. She believes that the main thing that keeps a silence from feeling powerful is when you stop projecting outward. "We retreat into internal conversations, thinking 'Oh God, I don't know what to say next,' so we've broken the connection by not being there with the other person," she says. "I think all bad silences are versions of that, of breaking a connection between the two people." Consequently, she firmly dismisses my suggestion that I might start inserting meaningful silences by pausing to check my phone: "You haven't left a silence, you've done an action, which is the same as words."

Her beginner's advice is simple: "The initial step is not to whip in immediately with the next question. When we do that we often miss the plot."

If even that feels daunting, she says, just remember that no "awkward" silence is as long as it feels: "If someone timed it for you, it would probably be about three-quarters of a second," she says. "What people think has been a horribly long silence never is, ever."

LUCY BALLANTYNE

A Fine Line

Earning (and wearing) one's stripes has not
always been black and white.

Photograph: Courtesy of Gemeentemuseum Den Haag and Sol LeWitt

The humble stripe has something of a checkered past. In his colorful and illuminating history of stripes, *The Devil's Cloth*, Michel Pastoureau reveals the hidden history of this simple pattern.

Stripes on clothing can be seen in mural paintings and various other creative works as early as the year 1000. Historically, they were a pejorative symbol that was used to mark out any and all characters who transgressed the social order in some way. This has, over time, included those who had been condemned (criminals), the infirm (lepers), the inferior (servants), the dishonorable (prostitutes) and the damned (non-Christians).

The medieval belief that stripes were inherently evil spread from the realm of symbolism into reality. When the Carmelite order of Christianity arrived in Paris in 1254, scandal erupted. The striped brethren's cloaks were considered so deviant from the cloaks of any other Christian order that they immediately became subject to ridicule and abuse. So much so that in 1295, Pope Boniface VIII banned striped cloaks for monks of all religious orders. But even before medieval times, plenty of texts specified a ban on clothes that were striped or even just bicolored. Brightly colored stripes were deemed particularly offensive—gaudy and unseemly.

Just as scholars debate the reasons behind the original negative perceptions of stripes, so too do they debate why attitudes ultimately changed. One theory is that toward the end of the Middle Ages, as towns in northern Italy were recovering from a late outbreak of the plague, young people celebrated by indulging in what was considered excessive and transgressive dressing—wearing stripes.

Meanwhile, some historians claim that the acceptance of stripes can be traced to zoologists' changing impressions of the zebra. The black-and-white striped animal was no longer considered a wild donkey, but instead a harmonious, elegantly dressed horse-like creature.

And Pastoureau describes a third possible theory: Stripes made the move from "diabolic to domestic" as they became typical on uniforms given to servants and various domestic staff. They then became aristocratic, and eventually, at the beginning of the first period of romanticism in the 18th century, wearing stripes became fashionable.

In the first decade of the 20th century, stripes finally hit peak chic. As going to the beach became less and less an aristocratic pastime, and instead something all could enjoy, stripes became a popular way to adorn beachwear. But even then, stripes only held a certain fashion cachet if they were colored against white.

We still haven't entirely shed our stripe hang-ups. Consider, for example, the stripes on a prisoner's uniform, which seem to depict the bars of a prison cell. And even now, the striped shirt isn't so black and white; something as simple as the cut of the fabric and the width of the lines can speak to the wearer's taste, location, even occupation.

SEAN MICHAELS

How to Listen to Jazz

An award-winning music writer on learning to appreciate a sudden skronk as much as a beautiful trill.

Nobody knows where the word "jazz" originated. It feels today like something that's always been. A vivid monosyllable—like dawn, or ash. Like the color blue. It might come from the French word *jaser*, chitchat, or from their word for hunting, *chasser*. It might have been invented by Titanic-era baseball players, who called their wobbliest pitches "jazz balls." Many scholars tie "jazz" to "jasm," an archaic term for energy, spirit or semen.

Somehow all of these explanations feel true. Jazz is dirty and spiritual; it's playful talk and murderous pursuit; it's a dancing object as it moves through the air.

It can also be painfully dull. While "jazz" is hot-blooded and beautiful, "jazzy" is almost always flaccid and false. At its worst, or to the heedless listener, jazz music can seem like empty frippery, saxes doing aerobics. A combo in the corner of a restaurant, soundtracking your charcuterie platter. Background music.

I was 15 when I learned that jazz was kindling—it can burst into fire. I had followed some friends to a festival concert, outdoors on a summer night. It was a mostly gray-haired crowd, so they let us scurry to the front; we sat down cross-legged before the stage. Wynton Marsalis came out with a great, shining big band. I was excited but to be honest, I was also ready for frippery. I was ready for aerobics. But what I heard instead was like dawn, ash or the color blue: profound, simple, irrefutable. Marsalis, playing trumpet, invented phrases out of thin air. And the Lincoln Center Orchestra, with horns held high, jousted with him. Their solos amplified and defied the melodies—raveling and unraveling them. For the first time, I was *seeing* jazz: the glances between musicians, the grins. This couldn't possibly fade into the background. It was for the foreground, with the volume up.

It's fashionable now to talk about mindfulness. *Stay present, we tell ourselves, try to stay present, for a few minutes at least.* Jazz is a music of unfurling nows, a genre built upon improvisation—and mindfulness is at the heart of improv. Each musician tries to manifest that very instant, whether it's as a sudden skronk or as a beautiful trill. Learning to love jazz is about learning to follow these changes, experiencing each solo as it happens. Any of us can bob along with Louis Armstrong's balladeering. Can we also slow our hearts down to Bill Evans' "Peace Piece"? Can we burst into bloom to John Coltrane's "Welcome"?

A lot of the time, playing jazz comes down to finding the right note. Landing on a perfect, unpredictable frequency—a coda that completes a thought, or a change that transforms it. Charlie Parker, the father of bebop, practiced scales until he could skip from one to any other, like a person who speaks a thousand languages and knows every possible *mot juste*. The Bad Plus's Ethan Iverson will touch a chord on his piano and change all the lighting in a room; Art Blakey would add a drum fill and make your breath catch in your throat.

But when there are too many right notes, jazz gets "jazzy" fast. This is also a music of wrong notes. Thelonious Monk called it trying to find "the right mistakes." Sometimes a sharp, flat or dissonant note is the choice that makes a musical phrase feel bittersweet or true. Sometimes it's what makes it come alive—something new, unimaginable. This is how the singer and trumpet player Chet Baker made his lonely music, but it's also how certain jazz gets to be so rowdy and impolite—from the raucous meditations of Nina Simone to Sun Ra's free-wheeling wizardry, preening and passing gas.

Too few wrong notes and jazz becomes mannered; too many and it's just noise. The listener, thankfully, doesn't have to work out the balance. The listener merely has to listen.

Nahanaeli Schelling

From finding beauty in the dryness of data, a business is born.

Nahanaeli Schelling spends her days looking for reason in rhythm. In New York, the Swiss-born software developer is working on a project that blends her greatest interest with her strongest skill: music and research. Finetunes is a music discovery tool that will allow its users to look deeper into the music industry and discover the often-uncredited people working behind the scenes—the producers, mixers and studio musicians. Right now, Schelling is knee-deep in data input and currently in prototype, but she doesn't mind. The drive behind her business mirrors her approach to navigating life: probing beyond the surface to uncover hidden truths.

What do you find most satisfying in daily life? I enjoy problem-solving. There needs to be some progress for it to feel like a good day for me. If I finish a task, then I want to know whether it was successful or not. If it wasn't, I want to know how to solve it. If it is, then I'm look-

ing at the next step. Either way, it's checking something off a to-do list that creates five more to-do items.

There must be downsides to being so gung-ho? It's hard to find a balance when you're working during the day and trying to work on your own projects at night. You need to make sure those projects are fun and you're enjoying them. That way, you start to see them as exploring or learning. I try to not be too hard on myself. I have different priorities than I did five years ago.

How so? When you're younger, there's a feeling that everything is going to be okay—no matter what: "I'm young, I'm alive and I've got my life ahead of me." That's still the case, but now it's more like, "Everything is going to be okay, if I make it okay."

Your work includes a lot of data science. Does that appeal to you? Data means nothing on its own— it's just a bunch of numbers. Its

only value is in what you do with it, so I guess it's more about context. With music, for example, you have all these numbers about how many people listen to your songs. The context is: Do they listen to the whole song? Do they listen on repeat? Where are they when they listen? You need to know the right questions to ask to avoid personal bias.

That seems like a good life lesson. I seek the truth and try to understand it. If someone says something that seems like an assumption, it's almost a public service to make them dive into it and look at the data. I won't ever just accept something because you heard it somewhere, or it's what you think. That's a standard that I hold my friends to, and what I think is missing in the media today. The only place to dive deep is through conversations with other people and with your friends. I feel lucky to have a group of people around me who are willing to engage.

Nahanaeli is using data from Frank Ocean's album *Blonde* to build the prototype for Finetunes. Here, she wears a top by Bally.

Photograph: Matthew Sprout, Styling: Debbie Hsieh, Hair and Makeup: Hiro Yonemoto

Reasons for raising your glass.

CHARMAINE LI
Chin Chin

Almost every country has its own drinking customs. In China, it's common to hold a glass below those of one's elders and superiors when toasting. In Sweden, songs are favored over simply saying *skål*.

Whether it's raising a glass before a meal or to celebrate a special occasion, toasting as a symbolic act to honor a moment has persevered throughout the ages. Some people perform the ritual as a mark of good manners, while others see the tradition as an important part of their cultural heritage. Regardless of the reason, toasting has become a way to inject a sense of respect and camaraderie into a social gathering.

Although no one knows the exact origins of toasting, what we do know is that celebrations involving alcohol date back to the Neolithic period. "The term 'toast'—the act of raising a glass during a festive celebration—gained popularity in the medieval times," explains Carolyn Panzer, director of corporate social responsibility for international alcoholic beverage company Diageo. "The name comes from the act of dropping a literal piece of spiced or charred bread into a cup or bowl of wine, either as a kind of hors d'oeuvre or to make the wine taste better."

Nearly half the world's population still performs toasting traditions, according to research by Diageo. Depending on where you are, the etiquette and significance of toasting can vary in form and intensity. In Japan, drinking is a social ritual linked closely to business and work and is taken very seriously. The important thing to remember is to wait for someone to say "cheers," or *kanpai*, before clinking glasses and taking your first sip. When it comes to German toasts, maintaining eye contact with each person you clink glasses with and saying *prost* or *zum wohl* is a crucial part of the custom. Meanwhile, drinkers in the UK and Hungary tend to be happy with simply hoisting glasses during a toast, rather than touching rims.

"Over time, toasting traditions have been passed down through generations for many different reasons," says Panzer. "Toasting in previous centuries was governed by a complex hierarchical etiquette. At social gatherings, glasses of wine were raised to the king, to each and every guest, and to lists of absent friends." Although toasting is a bit more flexible these days, the convivial ritual seems to be more important than ever as a symbolic act of goodwill and solidarity when sharing a drink.

Photograph: Alisa Aiv

BOTTOMS UP

by Molly Mandell

Selecting glassware is a small but significant task. Size, shape and texture work together and affect the drinking experience. To preserve the bubbles, highballs made with tonics or sodas are best served in narrow glasses like the Level glasses (top) designed by Ctrlzak for Luisaviaroma. Elsewhere, cordial glasses—known as pony glasses—are used for serving digestifs, specifically after-dinner liqueurs to sip as the evening winds down. Even in its smallest iteration, Ultima Thule glassware by Iittala in collaboration with Finnish designer Tapio Wirkkala (middle), is one of the most iconic. Finally, glass artist František Vízner and Czech brand Bomma have modernized the champagne bowl (bottom)—the vessel of choice for French nobility who, instead of savoring champagne, treated it more like a shot of whiskey.

EMILY NATHAN

Mover and Shaper

A celebrated sculptor and the matriarch of modern dance: the story of an unlikely power couple.

The little-known partnership between Isamu Noguchi and Martha Graham resides in a comfortable realm of reciprocal invention: art as an extension of art. Graham, born to a strict Presbyterian family in Pittsburgh in 1894, is widely considered the mother of modern dance; she revolutionized the physical vocabulary of the art form, translating primal human expression into movement and exploring the beauty of body language. A renegade and a pioneer—her influence is comparable to that of Picasso over the course of modern art—she incorporated every aspect of the dancing space into her choreography, using the stage, the floor and even props as elements as essential to her performance as her own appendages.

Noguchi, born in Los Angeles and raised in Japan, was a sculptor and designer whose commitment to spare simplicity—and a nothing-but-the-essentials ethos—was matched by a lifelong interest in making art that could and should be used.

It was in 1929, when Graham commissioned Noguchi to create two portrait heads, that their stories first intersected. Six years later, Graham realized that her innovative choreography might be better showcased by an equally striking backdrop, and she asked her friend to design the set for her solo dance, *Frontier*. Over the next three decades, Noguchi created some 20 sets for Graham's dances, sometimes erasing the distinction between set and prop. The stage, it turned out, was an invaluable canvas for him: It taught him that space, like any material, is itself a volume that can be dealt with sculpturally.

"So much of my life has been bound artistically with Isamu Noguchi," Graham told *The New York Times* at the time of Noguchi's death. "I feel the world has lost an artist who, like a shaman, has translated myths of all our lives into living memory. The works he created for my ballets brought to me a new vision, a new world of space and the utilization of space. Isamu, as I do, always looked forward and not to the past. My sense of loss is accentuated by the projects we had yet to accomplish—a set for my new ballet in the spring, and an exhibition of our works together that was to celebrate his 85th birthday in September, which now I hope will continue as a tribute to Isamu's continuing vision and power."

Sculptors and dancers are not often seen as natural collaborators, but Graham and Noguchi embodied two approaches to the same idea: They believed that collaboration was not only important but inevitable. For her, it took place between body and prop, space and limb, floor and foot. Noguchi, likewise, sought to liberate sculpture from the remote, exclusive confines of "fine art" and bring it into the realm of human life—to wed the values of aesthetics with those of function.

tf

Language: Portuguese. *Pronunciation:* "Dez-zen-ras-can-so." *Etymology:* From *des* meaning "un" and *enrascar* meaning "to entangle."

Meaning: Translating to "disentanglement," *desenrascanço* is a kind of Portuguese MacGyverism. It's the art of finding a solution to a problem out of left field, without the skills or resources one would usually require. It's artful disentanglement from a problem: throwing together a costume right before a party using the clothes already hanging in your wardrobe, propping up a wobbly table leg using the novel in your bag, or just about anything you do with duct tape.

Desenrascanço is imaginative resourcefulness when you need it most. It's a celebration less of the careful planning that comes before a situation arises, and more of the creative management of that situation as it happens. It's an indication of a more spontaneous approach to life—there's no need to concern yourself with unnecessary planning and detail when you feel confident that any problem you might encounter is solvable with the skills you already have, and the things you already own.

Some say desenrascanço is a distinctly Portuguese virtue. There are examples of businesses from other European nations moving their offices to Lisbon because the Portuguese are seen as more likely to employ desenrascanço when confronted with a professional problem. This kind of lateral thinking is emphasized in the Portuguese education system, too, especially in the country's universities.

Use: Desenrascanço is a common colloquial word in Portugal, and speaks to a way of being that emphasizes thinking outside the box and trusting one's instinct. The powerful and radical implication of desenrascanço is the notion that you have everything you could ever need inside of you already. If you're flexible and nimble, everything else is just extraneous detail—the latest gadget or tool is no substitute for an open, creative mind. No solution is outside of reach for a person determined to find it. Desenrascanço is a word for anyone who already knows this to be true, but also for anyone who needs to be reminded of the power and potential of their instincts.

LUCY BALLANTYNE

Word: Desenrascanço

Forget *hygge*: Uncertain times call for problem-solving the Portuguese way.

Toronto-based artist Corey Moranis has mastered the exact opposite of desenrascanço. Her knot sculptures are hand-twisted into intricate shapes using clear acrylic rods.

Payam Sharifi

Wall-to-wall: The artist on his decade-long exploration of Eurasia.

Since 2006, art collective Slavs and Tatars has presented a distinctive and kaleidoscopic vision of Eurasia—a geography that co-founder Payam Sharifi prefers to define as "the area east of the former Berlin Wall and west of the Great Wall of China." Over the last, complicated decade, for example, the collective's multidisciplinary projects have oscillated between the outlandish and the poignant: It has translated satirical 1930s cartoons from Azerbaijan, documented unlikely confluences in Iran and Poland's economic, social, political, religious and cultural histories, and examined the sacred role of language on more than one occasion. Slavs and Tatars' body of work even includes an adaptation of the *Flashdance* track "She's a Maniac" into "She's Armenian" (replacing the struggles of an aspiring dancer with those of the Armenian diaspora). Here, ahead of a new retrospective, Sharifi reflects on the last 10 years.

Previously, Slavs and Tatars' members were scattered across the globe. Now that you're all living in Berlin, has it had an impact on your practice? There's a flexibility in not having a studio in this line of research-based work. But I guess it was inevitable that we would end up with a studio—we have professionalized over the years. It's unsexy, but it allows us to focus. Berlin has a strategic advantage over other cities in its research resources. It has the breadth of libraries of a former Eastern capital because of its history, but also the volumes that I would find in Washington, D.C. Here, I find it all in one place.

Books are one of your biggest outputs. What significance do they hold? There's something very sacred about books; they can have a talismanic quality. When you go to someone's house, the first thing you see on the coffee table is a monograph of the artists they like or have collected—it's like a support material. What we try to do is the opposite. One of the reasons we're so fond of books is that they can be so accessible. Ours are not precious. They are books that you can take to your bathtub and read, and it's no big deal if they get wet. All of our installations—expensive, delicate, precious—are just a premise to bring people back to the books.

I hear you're opening a pickle bar. Our newest work is about the idea of souring—the politics behind fermentation. Pickling is kind of cool and fermentation has become hip again. And it originates in Central Asia and eastern Europe amongst Slavic and Turkic peoples. We're opening a pickle bar to be able to engage with the politics of pickling, beyond the arts institution, in the hospitality sector.

How much of a role does satire play in your work? There's something generous about humor. The ideal form is welcoming, a sort of laughing at oneself—an icebreaker. It can be a disarming way for us to allow access to a subject matter that would otherwise strike somebody as distant or frightening. But it can also be more than that. There's a great book, *Domination and the Arts of Resistance* by James C. Scott about the idea of "infrapolitics." A play on the word "infrared," it describes the politics that are there but that you can't see. It's the rumors, the jokes, the things that are hushed or whispered at home—the underbelly of politics beyond marching in the street, manifestos and policy acts. It's folk politics. Each joke is a tiny revolution.

Does the role of satire hold more significance today than it used to? The world is a very different place from when Slavs and Tatars started, in unexpected and unfortunate ways. The natural desire, of course, is to have your sphere of activity and your audience widen as opposed to narrow. But the world has been radicalized so much, and that presents a challenge for us: How do we sharpen our language appropriately?

Are you between a rock and hard place? A very important thing in art is to disrespect and respect at the same time. In order to disrespect your source, you have to respect it—you have to be familiar. The Western idea of criticism is always from a distance. But there's a way of critiquing through complete intimacy. Imagine critiquing something through a bear hug. We ask very stupid questions about very smart subject matters.

You're a decade into your practice. Are you asking questions about your own work? We're marking 10 years with a series of exhibitions—a sort of a midcareer survey that's traveling from Warsaw to Tehran, and then to Istanbul, Vilnius and Dresden. The challenge is to make sure that the work is never the end point. That sounds very

Payam co-founded Slavs and Tatars with Kasia Korczak in 2006. Since then, the art collective has exhibited in some of the world's most celebrated museums including the Centre Pompidou in Paris, Berlin's Hamburger Bahnhof and the Museum of Modern Art in New York.

Photograph: Marsý Hild Þórsdóttir

cliché—but no matter how good the work is, it shouldn't self-reflect. It's not a black hole. It should ping-pong somewhere else.

Did it hold any personal significance to exhibit in Tehran recently? Absolutely. Iran is one of the four countries I feel devoted to and where I've spent a lot of time. It's also important in a professional sense, however, because certain places like Turkey, Poland or Iran have a different understanding of our work.

Who do you see as your audience? One of the things that I'm most proud of is that we have a community of people interested in our work that is not normally interested in contemporary art. That's important to me—that we're not attracting only the specialist, but also the generalist, the layman. It's like how Chekhov was a doctor but is remembered as a writer. Maybe it's the release of professional constraints that allows people to have a more interesting take on what is not their primary source of income. They are people who are studying different subject matters and that are able to start from a different point of departure.

Do you have any hobbies of your own? My parents raised me saying, "Make sure that you wake up every morning passionate about what you're doing." We're fortunate to be able to make a living doing what we love. But it's not enough: The real challenge is not just to have an interest in a line of work, but to actually have a life that is equally as interesting and distinct from that work. The people I most admire—and I can count them on one hand—are those whose work is compelling, but whose life is even more so.

Who were your role models while growing up? I was reading an interview recently with Nassim Nicholas Taleb, who wrote *The Black Swan*. He was asked who his role models were and he said he didn't have any, that he had anti-role models instead. In a sense, the Iranian community in Texas was important to me as an anti-role model in that it represented only a very thin layer of what Iranian culture could be. That was what pushed me to pursue other identities—to start Russian studies, to live in Russia and to learn Russian. And it was actually in and through Russia that I later became

interested in Iran beyond my Iranian ethnicity.

What type of community are you finding in Berlin? Each place, each move, each new experience, has its challenges. Language filters your experience, and the biggest challenge of moving to Berlin thus far is not being able to speak German. So I'm learning it. I prefer hanging out with older Germans rather than younger, coffee-drinking hipsters because 60-year-olds tell and teach me much more—not just linguistically, but culturally.

Does Slavs and Tatars have an overarching goal for its future? Our interests remain the same, but the question is how to deliver them differently. I think that's going to mean looking outside of the art world and outside of the expected context of art—the white cube, the gallery, the museum. It's not a coincidence that art is following the path that fashion followed, and cinema before it. Fashion is still important, but not nearly as much as it was 10 years ago. As soon as something is in the zeitgeist, it's on its way out. Maybe we'll soon say the same thing about art.

"We ask very stupid questions about very smart subject matters."

Payam was born and raised in Texas and has since lived in Paris, Moscow, New York and Tehran. Here, he is pictured in his home in Berlin.

Photograph: Marsý Hild Þórsdóttir

2
Features

Deep

Salvation from summer's stark and sweltering skies.

Shadows

Photography by Marsý Hild Þórsdóttir & Styling by Rose Forde

Previous page: Imade wears a dress and belt by Loewe and shoes by Missoni. Above: She wears a swimsuit by COS, top by Sunad and hat by Superduper from Luisaviaroma.

Below: She wears a dress by JW Anderson.

Left: Imade wears a dress by Joseph and a hat by Jacquemus. Below: She wears a dress and belt by Loewe and shoes by Missoni.

Imade wears a dress by Marni and a hat by Jacquemus.

Left: Imade wears a dress by Céline and swimwear by Stella McCartney. Above: She wears a jumpsuit by Hermès.

The Bin Shabibs

In a preview from our forthcoming book, *The Kinfolk Entrepreneur, Pip Usher* meets *Rashid* and *Ahmed Bin Shabib*—the twin brothers giving voice to the modern Middle East. *Photography by Alexander Wolfe*

Rashid Bin Shabib is seated behind his desk at the offices of *Brownbook*, the bimonthly Dubai-based periodical he launched with his twin brother, Ahmed. Wearing a *kandoura*, tousled dark curls bidding an escape from his white *thobe*, Rashid cuts a dashing figure. He's internationally educated and erudite, as comfortable in Emirati national dress as he is in slim-cut trousers and owl-shaped glasses. He looks around him and sees the Middle East and North Africa as a region rich in tradition and beauty. And yet, whenever he flicks

on the news, it's the same old story. Death. Destruction. Dark, heavy stuff. It's hard not to let it wear him down.

"You read it, and then see it reinforced and reappropriated. It becomes an echo chamber to some extent," he says of the mainstream media's myopic portrayal of the Middle East. "We're always hearing about topics of religion, tolerance, different value sets. That's important, without a doubt. But that agenda is not our fight. Our job here is to show the progressive and optimistic side of the region."

Cue *Brownbook*, the brothers' decade-old magazine that comes out of a desire to showcase a lesser-seen side of the Middle East that other media outlets largely ignore. Born and raised in the United Arab Emirates, the pair credit their grandfather—a businessman who later became Minister of Transport and Infrastructure—with instilling an academic interest in the evolving role of cities and society. Their mother, who raised them alone, was another powerful role model ("She's very liberal, open-minded, progres-

"*Instead of saying, 'All of this is wrong,' we rephrase it as, 'Here's what's going right.'*"

Both twins are interested in the urban development of Dubai. The first building they repurposed, Shelter, was nominated for an Aga Khan Award for Architecture.

sive," says Rashid). This conflation of interests and values can be seen on the pages of *Brownbook*, which describes itself as an urban guide to the Middle East and North Africa and unpacks the region's modern identity.

"In Bahrain, Algeria, Alexandria, in Tripoli, Abu Dhabi and Jeddah, of course there's normality," says Rashid. "Not only is there a sense of stability, but there are progressive ideologies and a beauty that's constantly evolving." A recent issue of *Brownbook* showcased culture in Palestine; on its website, an accompanying short film featured a Palestinian-Belizean politician reflecting on his life. It's an intimate and humanizing look at the ordinary—and extraordinary—individuals that make up the region and its diaspora communities. Or, as Rashid grandly declares, it's "a periodical that audits the evolution of a culture."

The brothers have witnessed the transformation of Dubai from small town to shiny metropolis. With the speed of a California gold-rush town, Dubai's fortunes skyrocketed when crude oil was discovered in the 1960s. Frenetic development followed, an accompanying boom in real estate, finance, tourism and retail drawing a wave of migrants from around the world. Today, 83 percent of Dubai's population is expatriate—a startling statistic that helps explain Rashid and Ahmed's desire to map out who they are in a "post-modern, post-Oriental, very complex world."

The brothers launched *Brownbook* in 2006—a bold move considering that many better-established magazines were disintegrating into financial disarray. But their decision was driven by practicalities; as Rashid explains, a magazine was the most practical vehicle for their ambitious storytelling. "Magazines are still the most progressive medium in which you can compile and build a narrative about a specific topic," he says.

Even when dealing with subjects as complex as Palestine—the mere mention of which can send people into the political trenches—the Bin Shabibs are careful to remain neutral. They see the confrontational tactics employed in other countries as counterproductive in light of the more subtle social codes of the Gulf. "The whole whistle-blowing, finger-pointing style of journalism is well positioned in a liberal, democratic so-

> *"Not only is there a sense of stability, but there are progressive ideologies and a beauty that's constantly evolving."*

ciety," says Rashid. "Whereas in a region that is extremely autocratic and driven by *sheikhism*, whistle-blowing and finger-pointing is not seen as the norm. It's a Western approach toward journalism."

To illustrate his point, he recounts the story of a friend who was beaten up as a teenager. When the attacker was let go because of his father's political connections, the victim's mother went to the ruler and read a poem that she had written praising the ruler's sense of justice. The ruler asked why she had chosen that piece, the sticky situation was explained and the attacker was subsequently punished. Justice prevailed—but it was reached through a circuitous route of artistic expression, flattery and gently applied pressure. "Unspoken language is still very much embedded in our culture," says Rashid. He believes that *Brownbook*'s success lies in its intuitive approach to such etiquette, the resolutely optimistic slant of its stories and its encouragement of readers to look at what's working in other countries in the region as an impetus for progress in their own. "Instead of saying,

'All of this is wrong,' we rephrase it as, 'Here's what's going right,'" he adds.

Alongside *Brownbook*, the brothers explore what they term "cultural engineering" in its many guises—publishing, exhibitions, and most notably through urban development projects. Both brothers studied economics and property development at Suffolk University in Boston, before completing degrees in urbanism at the University of Oxford. The imposing architecture and storied histories of their alma maters left a lasting impression that has guided their ideas to this day. "Boston is Boston, whether you like it or not. It imposes itself on you and you enjoy it for what it is," says Rashid of the city's crusty New England temperament and grand Georgian architecture. "When you come back to Dubai, you start to think about the beauty of the past."

Their fascination with the importance of civic spaces led to the duo's first architectural undertaking around the same time that *Brownbook* launched. They settled on repurposing an old nail factory in Al Quoz, a largely indus-

trial area of Dubai that *The New York Times* once deemed "the gritty opposite of glamorous." A warehouse space was transformed into a co-working campus called Shelter. The idea was to bring small business owners together; local entrepreneurs and freelancers were enticed to its desks by free rent, a relaxed, open-plan layout and regular networking events. On a deeper level, it was a bid to forge community.

"I'm far more interested in how we can create spaces for people to come together, whether that's formed in a physical place or a non-physical one—as in being a member of a regional collective," says Ahmed. He points to their recent work at Al Khazzan Cadillac Park, an inner-city green space, in which they launched a free public library with content curated by *Brownbook*. Again, the aim is to foster meaningful interaction and, Ahmed hopes, to encourage these exchanges to take place outside of Dubai's ubiquitous shopping malls. "It brings people together to meet around productive social experiences," he says. "It allows people to meet, create workshops, set

Overleaf: The twins founded The Magazine Shop—the first in Dubai to sell independent magazines.

This table was custom-made by Case Design Studio.

up markets and so forth without the need to just consume."

When it comes to Dubai's metamorphosis, the brothers are gently mocking: "The agenda is eggs Benedict with protein shakes and kale salads," Rashid jokes of the city's fondness for the type of imported trends that are at odds with the genuine cultural movement they are seeking. "It would be more refreshing to see an authentic movement within Arabic literature," he adds, "Or craftsmanship in ornamentation. That's not happening."

But the twins aren't despairing. They know that it will take time to reconcile Dubai's swift globalization with its cultural heritage and traditions. For Ahmed, the Emirati national dress is a symbolic reminder of the enduring strength of the *khaleeji* (Gulf) identity. "Development came to the country at a late stage, so we entered the modern world with the past very visually present," he says. "If you look at a photograph from a G20 summit, every leader wears a suit or a pantsuit, but one person is still wearing the *kandoura*."

Ahmed is also heartened by the tolerance practiced between Emiratis and the city's expatriates. "I think kids in Dubai have more national holidays than in any other city," he says, citing the steady influx of Arabs, Iranians, Indians and Levantines over the past century, all of whom brought new customs. "This mix forced people to have a strong sense of empathy for one another in a way that I've not seen before in the region."

Open-minded and hopeful: These are words perhaps not usually applied to the Middle East. But then again, Western media tends not to look in the right places. In their battle to balance progress with tradition, Rashid and Ahmed document their region's complexity without trying to provide easy answers. They know there are none. "*Brownbook* and our other projects try to reinforce our identity to the world because that's what the rest of the world does—constantly reiterates its identity," Rashid says. "And that serves to reaffirm our identity within ourselves."

Excerpt:

Hope in the Dark

In her book *Hope in the Dark*, *Rebecca Solnit* offers a clarion call for anyone who has forgotten the lesson that history repeatedly reminds us: that change, be it personal or political, is never inevitable. It must be fought for.

"Memory produces hope in the same way that amnesia produces despair," the theologian Walter Brueggemann noted. It's an extraordinary statement, one that reminds us that though hope is about the future, grounds for hope lie in the records and recollections of the past. We can tell of a past that was nothing but defeats and cruelties and injustices, or of a past that was some lovely golden age now irretrievably lost, or we can tell a more complicated and accurate story, one that has room for the best and worst, for atrocities and liberations, for grief and jubilation.

A memory commensurate to the complexity of the past and the whole cast of participants, a memory that includes our power, produces that forward-directed energy called hope.

Amnesia leads to despair in many ways. The status quo would like you to believe it is immutable, inevitable and invulnerable, and lack of memory of a dynamically changing world reinforces this view. In other words, when you don't know how much things have changed, you don't see that they are changing or that they can change. Those who think that way don't remember raids on gay bars when being queer was illegal or rivers that caught fire when unregulated pollution peaked in the 1960s or that there were, worldwide, 70 percent more seabirds a few decades ago and very, very few homeless people in the United States before the economic shifts of the Reagan Revolution. Thus, they don't recognize the forces of change at work.

One of the essential aspects of depression is the sense that you will always be mired in this misery, that nothing can or will change. It's what makes suicide so seductive as the only visible exit from the prison of the present.

There's a public equivalent to private depression, a sense that the nation or the society rather than the individual is stuck. Things don't always change for the better, but they change, and we can play a role in that change if we act. Which is where hope comes in, and memory, the collective memory we call history.

The other affliction amnesia brings is a lack of examples of positive change, of popular power, evidence that we can do it and have done it. George Orwell wrote, "Who controls the past controls the future. Who controls the present controls the past." Controlling the past begins by knowing it; the stories we tell about who we were and what we did shape what we can and will do. Despair is also often premature: It's a form of impatience as well as of certainty.

My favorite comment about political change comes from Zhou En-lai, a high-ranking member of Chairman Mao's government. Asked, in the early 1970s, about his opinion of the French Revolution, he answered, "Too soon to tell." Some argue that he was talking about the insurrections of 1968, not the monarchy-toppling of 1789, but even then it demonstrates a generous and expansive perspective. To retain a sense that even four years later the verdict isn't in is to live with more open-minded uncertainty than most people now can tolerate.

News cycles tend to suggest that change happens in small, sudden bursts or not at all. Last June, the former army officer who murdered Chilean singer and political activist Victor Jara in 1973 was charged. More than 40 years had gone by; some stories take far longer than that to finish. The struggle to get women the vote took nearly three-quarters of a century. For a time people liked to announce that feminism had failed, as though the project of overturn-

ing millennia of social arrangements should achieve its final victories in a few decades, or as though it had stopped. Feminism is just starting, and its manifestations matter in rural Himalayan villages, not just first-world cities. Susan Griffin, a great writer in the present who was also an important part of 1970s feminism, recently remarked, "I've seen enough change in my lifetime to know that despair is not only self-defeating, it is unrealistic."

Other changes result in victories and are then forgotten. For decades, radicals were preoccupied with East Timor, brutally occupied by Indonesia from 1975 to 2002; the liberated country is no longer news. It won its liberty because of valiant struggle from within, but also because of dedicated groups on the outside who pressured and shamed the governments supporting the Indonesian regime. We could learn quite a lot from the remarkable display of power and solidarity and its eventual victory, but the whole struggle seems forgotten.

For decades, Peabody Western Coal Company mined coal on the Hopi/Navajo land at Black Mesa in ways that contaminated the air and drained vast amounts of water from the region. The fight against Black Mesa was a totemic struggle for indigenous sovereignty and environmental justice; in 2005, the mines were shut down, and the issue disappeared from the conversation. It was also a case of tenacious activism from within and good allies from without, prolonged lawsuits and perseverance.

We need litanies or recitations or monuments to these victories, so that they are landmarks in everyone's mind. More broadly, shifts in, say, the status of women are easily overlooked by people who don't remember that there was no recourse for exclusion, discrimination, workplace sexual harassment, most forms of rape and other crimes against women the legal system did not recognize or even countenanced a few decades ago. None of the changes were inevitable, either—people fought for them and won them.

People adjust without assessing the changes. As of 2014, Iowa gets 28 percent of its electricity from wind alone, not because someone in that conservative state declared death to all fossil fuel corporations or overthrew anyone or anything, but because it was a sensible and affordable option. Denmark, in the summer of 2015, achieved 140 percent of its electricity needs through wind generation (and sold the surplus to neighboring countries). Scotland has achieved renewable energy generation of 50 percent and set a goal of 100 percent by 2020. Thirty percent more solar was installed in 2014 than the year before in the United States, and renewables are becoming more affordable worldwide—in some places they are already cheaper than fossil-fueled energy. These incremental changes have happened quietly, and many people don't know they have begun, let alone exploded.

If there is one thing we can draw from where we are now and where we were then, it is that the unimaginable is ordinary, that the way forward is almost never a straight line you can glance down but a convoluted path of surprises, gifts and afflictions you prepare for by accepting your blind spots as well as your intuitions. Howard Zinn wrote in 1988—in what now seems like a lost world before so many political upheavals and technological changes arrived, "As this century draws to a close, a century packed with history, what leaps out from that history is its utter unpredictability." He was, back then, wondering at the distance we'd traveled from when the Democratic National Party Convention refused to seat blacks from Mississippi to when Jesse Jackson ran (a largely symbolic campaign) for president at a time most people thought they would never live to see a black family occupy the White House. In that essay, "The Optimism of Uncertainty," Zinn continues,

The struggle for justice should never be abandoned because of the apparent overwhelming power of those who have the guns and the money and who seem invincible in their determination to hold onto it. That apparent power has, again and again, proved vulnerable to moral fervor, determination, unity, organization, sacrifice, wit, ingenuity, courage, patience—whether by blacks in Alabama and South Africa, peasants in El Salvador, Nicaragua and Vietnam, or workers and intellectuals in Poland, Hungary and the Soviet Union itself.

Social, cultural or political change does not work in predictable ways or on predictable schedules. The month before the Berlin Wall fell, almost no one anticipated that the Soviet bloc was going to disintegrate all of a sudden (thanks to many factors, including the tremendous power of civil society, nonviolent direct action and hopeful organizing going back to the 1970s), any more than anyone, even the participants, foresaw the impact that the Arab Spring or Occupy Wall Street or a host of other great uprisings would have. We don't know what is going to happen, or how or when, and that very uncertainty is the space of hope.

Those who doubt that these moments matter should note how terrified the authorities and elites are when they erupt. That fear signifies their recognition that popular power is real enough to overturn regimes and rewrite the social contract. And it often has. Sometimes your enemies know what your friends can't believe. Those who dismiss these moments because of their imperfections, limitations or incompleteness need to look harder at what joy and hope shine out of them and what real changes have

"If people find themselves living in a world in which some hopes are realized and some joys are incandescent and some boundaries between individuals and groups are lowered, even for an hour or a day or several months, that matters. Memory of joy and liberation can become a navigational tool, an identity, a gift."

emerged because of them, even if not always in the most obvious or recognizable ways.

And everything is flawed, if you want to look at it that way. The analogy that has helped me most is this: In Hurricane Katrina, hundreds of boat-owners rescued people—single moms, toddlers, grandfathers—stranded in attics, on roofs, in flooded housing projects, hospitals and school buildings. None of them said, *I can't rescue everyone, therefore it's futile; therefore my efforts are flawed and worthless,* though that's often what people say about more abstract issues in which, nevertheless, lives, places, cultures, species, rights are at stake. They went out there in fishing boats and rowboats and pirogues and all kinds of small craft, some driving from as far as Texas and eluding the authorities to get in, others refugees themselves working within the city. There was bumper-to-bumper boat-trailer traffic—the celebrated Cajun Navy—going *toward* the city the day after the levees broke. None of those people said, *I can't rescue them all.* All of them said, *I can rescue someone, and that's work so meaningful and important I will risk my life and defy the authorities to do it.* And they did.

Change is rarely straightforward. Sometimes it's as complex as chaos theory and as slow as evolution. Even things that seem to happen suddenly arise from deep roots in the past or from long-dormant seeds. A young man's suicide triggers an uprising that inspires other uprisings, but the incident was a spark; the bonfire it lit was laid by activist networks and ideas about civil disobedience and by the deep desire for justice and freedom that exists everywhere.

It's important to ask not only what those moments produced in the long run but what they were in their heyday. If people find themselves living in a world in which some hopes are realized and some joys are incandescent and some boundaries between individuals and groups are lowered, even for an hour or a day

or several months, that matters. Memory of joy and liberation can become a navigational tool, an identity, a gift.

Paul Goodman famously wrote, "Suppose you had the revolution you are talking and dreaming about. Suppose your side had won, and you had the kind of society that you wanted. How would you live, you personally, in that society? Start living that way now!" It's an argument for tiny and temporary victories, and for the possibility of partial victories in the absence or even the impossibility of total victories. Total victory has always seemed like a secular equivalent of paradise: a place where all the problems are solved and there's nothing to do, a fairly boring place. The absolutists of the old left imagined that victory would, when it came, be total and permanent, which is practically the same as saying that victory was and is impossible and will never come. It is, in fact, more than possible. It is something that has arrived in innumerable ways, small and large and often incremental, but not in that way that was widely described and expected. So victories slip by unheralded. Failures are more readily detected.

And then every now and then, the possibilities explode. In these moments of rupture, people find themselves members of a "we" that did not until then exist, at least not as an entity with agency and identity and potency; new possibilities suddenly emerge, or that old dream of a just society reemerges and—at least for a little while—shines. Utopia is sometimes the goal. It's often embedded in the moment itself, and it's a hard moment to explain, since it usually involves hardscrabble ways of living, squabbles and eventually disillusion and factionalism—but also more ethereal things: the discovery of personal and collective power, the realization of dreams, the birth of bigger dreams, a sense of connection that is as emo-

tional as it is political, and lives that change and do not revert to older ways even when the glory subsides.

Sometimes the earth closes over this moment and it has no obvious consequences; sometimes empires crumble and ideologies fall away like shackles. But you don't know beforehand. People in official institutions devoutly believe they hold the power that matters, though the power we grant them can often be taken back; the violence commanded by governments and militaries often fails, and nonviolent direct-action campaigns often succeed.

The sleeping giant is one name for the public; when it wakes up, when we wake up, we are no longer only the public: We are civil society, the superpower whose nonviolent means are sometimes, for a shining moment, more powerful than violence, more powerful than regimes and armies. We write history with our feet and with our presence and our collective voice and vision. And yet, and of course, everything in the mainstream media suggests that popular resistance is ridiculous, pointless or criminal, unless it is far away, was long ago, or ideally both. These are the forces that prefer the giant remain asleep.

Together we are very powerful, and we have a seldom-told, seldom-remembered history of victories and transformations that can give us confidence that yes, we can change the world because we have many times before. You row forward looking back, and telling this history is part of helping people navigate toward the future. We need a litany, a rosary, a sutra, a mantra, a war chant of our victories. The past is set in daylight, and it can become a torch we can carry into the night that is the future.

An extended version of this essay appears in the third edition of Rebecca Solnit's Hope in the Dark: Untold Histories, Wild Possibilities, *published in 2016 by Haymarket Books.*

LARTIGUE

Words by Asher Ross

Jacques Henri Lartigue was a wealthy bon vivant whose photography was guided by the pleasure principle. With his camera, Lartigue doted on the somatic beauty of French summers—the sporting life, fast cars and the splash of swimmers at play. Strange, then, that the world has so long neglected his work in color. Perhaps it's a remnant of midcentury photography's black-and-white orthodoxy, which Lartigue merrily defied. Contemplating an orange in a letter to Anaïs Nin, for example, he once wrote, "It's about showing that it shines in the sun [...] that it's not a dead object." *Lartigue: Life in Color*, along with its excellent introductory essay by Martine Ravache, aims to open the blinds on Lartigue's full legacy and let the sunlight come rushing in.

Florette
(1969)

Florette, Piozzo
(1960)

Florette, Piozzo
(1960)

Florette, Opio
(1960)

Florette dans la Morgan
(1954)

Carven, Agay
(1962)

J.

Prodigal. Dark. Incandescent: A short chronicle of the life of an English cellist.

Words by Suzanne Snider

du

Pré

When Jacqueline du Pré was four years old, she heard a pleasing sound on the radio. She later explained, "I liked it so much that I asked my mother to get me the thing that made that sound." Without hesitation, Iris du Pré bought her daughter a full-size cello, one so large that Jackie had to stand and wrap her arms around the instrument's body to play it.

Most biographies of musical prodigies begin with such precocious anecdotes. These would be forgettable stories were they not, in hindsight, early evidence of artistic genius—if, for example, Jacqueline hadn't become one of the greatest cellists in the world,.

For 15 years—from 1961 to 1976—Jacqueline seduced music lovers with her virtuosic performances and initiated thousands of fans previously unmoved by classical music. Her talent for converting the latter to superfandom lay both in her vibrant interpretations and in the glamour that seemed to surround her personal life. Her wild success along with that of her pianist husband made the pair the perfect protagonists for the musical soap opera that unfolded. Jacqueline became a hero to young musicians, especially to women, but her life would

take a tragic turn when she was diagnosed with multiple sclerosis at the age of 28—and died at 42.

Iris du Pré felt confident about her investment in Jacqueline's cello from the start. "I knew she was musical because she could tap rhythms that I tapped for her before she was a year old, and she could also sing in tune before she could talk." A former concert pianist herself, Iris taught piano and eurhythmic movement lessons in the family living room while raising three children 20 miles south of London. Jacqueline's father, Derek du Pré, was assistant editor of *The Accountant* magazine.

Jacqueline entered The London Violoncello School when she was six years old. The school taught girls to wrap their legs around the cellos while other schools made girls play more primly, in sidesaddle. The method was a good match for Jacqueline, whose lack of physical inhibition when she played—described in turn as "floppy" and "flamboyant"—was an early and enduring trademark of her performances. In videos, her head and torso frequently jerk about, moved by her own music.

At age 10, Jacqueline began to study under musician William

The notion of a "popular cellist" may sound oxymoronic, but Jacqueline had appeal beyond the concert-going crowd.

Jacqueline's mother, Iris, wrote and illustrated short musical compositions for her daughter, slipping them under her pillow as she slept. When Jacqueline woke up to a new song, she would grab the music and run for her cello before getting dressed.

Previous spread's photograph: Brian Seed / Lebrecht. Left photograph: David Farrell/Lebrecht. Right photograph: Brian Seed/Lebrecht

Jacqueline was only 20 years old when she performed Edward Elgar's Cello Concerto in E minor, Op. 85 with the London Symphony Orchestra in 1965. The two—du Pré and the concerto—are historically intertwined, each serving to underscore the exceptionality of the other.

Pleeth, who managed to teach the young musician technique without quashing her joy and curiosity. The following year, Jacqueline won the famed Suggia Gift Award, beating out competitors almost twice her age. Recommending Jacqueline for the award, Pleeth wrote that she was "the most outstanding cellistic and musical talent that I have met so far, to which she adds incredible maturity of mind." The prize covered six years of cello lessons and brought Jacqueline into contact with an expanding audience. Five weeks before she turned 16, Jacqueline made her debut at London's Wigmore Hall. By that time, Jacqueline had already dropped out of school.

Jacqueline's impressive ascent added to the pleasure with which audiences experienced her music. Like an Olympic athlete, she represented the best of human ability. The notion of a "popular cellist" may sound oxymoronic, but Jacqueline had appeal beyond the concert-going crowd. For some fans, her stock rose when she married Argentine-Israeli pianist Daniel Barenboim after six months of courtship. She converted to Judaism immediately (as much a gesture of love for her husband as it was to the many talented Jewish musicians with whom Jacqueline played). Equally thrilling, she successfully infiltrated an elite gang of male musicians (think Itzhak Perlman, Pinchas Zukerman and Yehudi Menuhin).

Jacqueline is best known for her performance of Edward Elgar's Cello Concerto in E minor, Op. 85. The concerto was composed after World War I in 1919 and was described as a war requiem. Jacqueline first performed it in 1965, and it would become one of her most popular recordings; filmmaker Christopher Nupen made *Jacqueline du Pré and the Elgar Cello Concerto*, a live concert film of Jacqueline playing the concerto with Barenboim and the New Philharmonia Orchestra.

"Listening to her perform the Elgar, in particular, the sense of nostalgia and yearning already present in that work, can take on a new dimension when considering the debilitating illness that was just around the corner," wrote Sarah Kirkup in a 2015 feature in *Gramophone*.

Jacqueline's biography often focuses on the well-worn tropes of "child prodigy" and illness narratives, but this negates much of what came in between—the sometimes banal but always significant details of which any life is made.

Originally from Devon, Iris du Pré was a musician with some record of accomplishment. Her talent as a pianist had brought about school scholarships and offers to travel and study. She was studying in Poland when she met Derek du Pré, who had come to Poland on vacation, carrying his accordion. Though Derek's family was more prosperous than Iris's, thanks to its perfume-making business, Iris had social graces, strength of character and talent. These made her an acceptable match for Derek, according to du Pré biographer Elizabeth Wilson. The couple had three children: Born on

January 26, 1945, Jacqueline was three years younger than her sister, Hilary, and three years older than her brother, Piers.

In 1948, the family of five moved to a suburb of London. Initially, it was Hilary who demonstrated remarkable musical talent. She started with the piano and then moved on to the flute. Peter Thomas, a high school friend of Jacqueline's, suggests that Jacqueline's musical superiority may have been exaggerated for the sake of the story: "[Hilary's] flute playing was extraordinary. Hilary had amazing body language and moved far more than Jackie did—she was a real snake charmer."

Discord seems almost inevitable given the overabundance of musical aspiration in the du Pré home, including Iris's deferred dreams. Much of her schedule revolved around the girls' lessons and competitions. And Iris served as Jacqueline's accompanist at concerts and competitions for 10 years, right up until her debut at Wigmore Hall, when Bill Pleeth hired Ernest Lush instead.

It's not clear when Jacqueline's career eclipsed Hilary's, but the consequences were chronicled in *A Genius in the Family*, an unflinching book written by Hilary and Piers, which served as the basis for the equally controversial film, *Hilary and Jackie*. The book caused waves for its portrayal of Jacqueline as depressed, manic and jealous. While the book and film highlight Jacqueline's flaws, Hilary emerges as both victim and hero—the housewife who evaded the misery of fame with a more humble life in the country, four children and no music career.

When the book came out, Jacqueline's colleagues defended her reputation, taking umbrage with the book's characterization of the cellist as selfish and manipulative and with the book's diminishment of music and musicianship. "What appears to have caused offense is not too little truth but too much honesty," Hilary argued. Specifically, the book revealed an affair between Jackie and Hilary's husband, Christopher Finzi, a ménage to which Hilary reluctantly consented.

Of course, writing a biography is inherently challenging, and Jacqueline repeatedly proves to be an elusive subject. Those who access Jacqueline's life through words may be confused and unduly distracted by minor discrepancies. Her story is necessarily musical and is best told through the music she left behind. Biographers and journalists can't even agree upon her physical appearance, for example. Descriptions of Jacqueline range wildly, including depictions of her as flamboyant, athletic, beautiful, larger than life, awkward, shy and dowdy.

Another point on which biographers don't agree is her feelings toward her cello. While Jacqueline is sometimes depicted as singularly focused and devoted, cellist Joan Dickson remembers a more melancholic Jacqueline who begged to stay in Dickson's spare bedroom and relax while her parents thought she was practicing. Referring to a friend who gave up the cello, Jacqueline confided to Dickson, "You know, that girl's lucky. She could give up music if she wants to. But I never could give it up because too many people spent too much money on me." She also once said in an interview, "I've never been a career demon. I love playing the cello and playing to people, but I have never wanted to do it every day and ev-

Jacqueline and Daniel Barenboim performed in Israel in the days leading up to the Six-Day War. Daniel recalls seeing tanks on the road returning from their final concert on June 5th. Shortly after the war ended, the couple wed in Jerusalem.

Photograph: David Farrell/Lebrecht

Aside from her siblings' memoir, *A Genius in the Family*, Jacqueline's life has been recounted in several biographies including one by Carol Easton, a close friend, and another by professional cellist Elizabeth Wilson.

ery hour of my life," though this is largely what she ended up doing.

When Jacqueline was 26 years old, she experienced occasional loss of feeling in her hands, which doctors dismissed variously as fatigue, stress and hysteria (for which she underwent psychoanalysis). After a two-year sabbatical, she returned to perform four concerts in 1973, which most fans viewed as her "comeback." She made it through three of those concerts before leaving the stage forever. During her final public performance, she played the Elgar Cello Concerto in London. By that time, she was having great difficulty with the bow and with basic tasks, like opening her cello case. She relied on sight as opposed to touch during that final performance to place her fingers and keep her bow in the correct position. The audience— without knowing her challenges— gave her a standing ovation.

Daniel Barenboim explained to one journalist, "Every doctor said something different. They couldn't agree on anything. This went on for 4½ years. Jackie and I knew something was terribly wrong—we just couldn't name it."

Ultimately, she was diagnosed with multiple sclerosis.

Post-diagnosis, Jacqueline had to decide what to do with a life that had been so narrowly defined. In one interview, she explained, "It's hard to try to rebuild something that feels worthwhile. So that's been my job, rebuilding. The only thing I have ever known about anything is playing the cello." She channeled her talents into teaching with mixed results. The fact was that "playing through students was the only way left of making music for her made the relationship almost unbearably difficult to deal with," explained Anssi Karttunen, a Finnish cellist and former du Pré student.

The end of Jacqueline's life was lonely, though students and friends continued to cycle through her home. Ironically, her accomplishments and wealth isolated her. Instead of being in a more social setting with other patients undergoing similar medical challenges, she was entirely dependent on friends and—in the end—a nurse named Ruth Cannings. Now the head of Arise Ministry in the UK, Cannings was actively evangelical during Jacqueline's decline.

Cannings purportedly told Jacqueline that "she would be cured if she turned to the Lord," and even her mother believed that Jacqueline's illness might be retribution for converting to Judaism. (Iris, Derek and Piers became born-again Christians at the end of Jacqueline's life.)

During Jacqueline's final years, her husband was busy giving 100 concerts a year. Unbeknownst to Jacqueline, he had also fathered two sons with a mistress. Despite his double life, many believe that Daniel was fully devoted to Jacqueline during this time, calling her nightly and returning to London to check on her. Her parents and siblings were largely absent. While some attributed her mother's distance to heartache, others saw it as disappointment—a failure of return on her investment. Jacqueline was surrounded by friends and her husband when she died.

Despite the brevity of her career, Jacqueline left behind 46 albums. And for young female musicians, in particular, she stands as a paragon, an unwitting feminist icon purely for her insistence on flamboyant expression and the legacy that came from its audacity.

Art of

A meal inspired by Alexander Calder, Cornelia Parker, Damien Hirst, Yayoi Kusama and Salvador Dalí.

Breakfast

Photography by Aaron Tilley, Set Design by Kyle Bean & Food Styling by Lucy-Ruth Hathaway

At Home With:
Roberto Baciocchi

Restrained in his work as an architect, *Roberto Baciocchi* likes to let loose at home. Strange and beautiful, his 700-year-old Tuscan villa conceals secret passageways, frescoed ceilings and a whole host of singular fixtures —from Gio Ponti chairs to garden gnomes. *David Plaisant* explores. *Photography by Marsý Hild Þórsdóttir*

The approach to architect Roberto Baciocchi's home is unassuming. The house occupies a street corner in the medieval core of Arezzo, the Tuscan city of his birth, where a tight, meticulously preserved urban fabric surrounds the property and conceals even a hint at what is inside.

At 71, Baciocchi has built his reputation on providing crisply modern, often monochrome interiors such as those he designed for Prada stores around the world. His home of 30 years, which he shares with his wife, Rosella, could not feel less minimal, however. Original in its use of space and layout, the 700-year-old Tuscan villa can seem labyrinthine; narrow stone staircases ascend a central tower, while concealed stairways descend into myriad chambers and antechambers.

Every room is filled with furniture spanning the centuries. And yet the house does not reflect the idiosyncrasies of an eccentric owner; Baciocchi is far too sober for that. Objects and fittings are intricately thought through. The architect is keen to point out that the house is a deeply personal odyssey that is most definitely not for show.

"I decided to buy this house because these spaces communicated something to me," says Baciocchi, who is seated on a semicircular midcentury couch that has been reupholstered in exquisite silvery gray antique velvet. "Can you imagine if this was all painted white?" he says looking up at the soft earthy tones of the frescoed ceiling of an intimately proportioned entrance room. "Imagine knocking through this or that wall, and perhaps having some architect say how the contemporary contrasts so well with the old," he continues, with a tone of lament (if not scorn). "Do that, and you might as well buy a different house!"

Predictability and unoriginality are nuisances that Baciocchi avoids at all costs. In the entrance room, for example, the level of detail and finish are particularly apparent. One wall is flanked with fitted wardrobes, the doors of which are embellished with the somber, abstract oil paintings of fellow *Aretino* (native of Arezzo) artist Giuseppe Friscia. They open with a gentle push to reveal softly lit mint-green linings, again in velvet. He explains, "I use velvet because it exalts colors, because of what it does to light, not just for the sake of using velvet." He also loves to use mirrors, and the adjoining bathroom (ceiling included) is covered in antique mirrored glass that he picked up at a Venice auction in the '70s. "What I detest most," says the architect with a big sigh, "is mediocrity."

Baciocchi may create clean, minimal interiors for his clients but his home is an extension of his personality—colorful, eclectic and proudly Italian.

"What I detest most," says the architect with a big sigh, "is mediocrity."

Baciocchi designed some of the
furniture in his home himself,
including the cherrywood table and
sideboard pictured here. In addition
to his architectural and interior work,
Baciocchi has designed tableware for
Milan's Nilufar Gallery and collections
for Tuscan chair company Quinti.

We make our way farther into the house—past ancient walls, at times three feet thick, and through diminutive doorways five centuries old. In a room with no external windows, more built-in wardrobes are fitted with paintings, this time of Rosella's father. A cheekier side of Baciocchi emerges as he reveals what is actually hidden behind its doors: a private nook, complete with fully-made single bed, mounted TV set and velvety, floral-print wallpaper. "My wife hates air-conditioning," he says. "But I love to have it on, so this is my home on summer nights."

In an en-suite bathroom, which contains an olive-green tub and matching basin and toilet ("late 1950s Italian, picked up in London"), a bronzed-glass shaving mirror affixed to the wall can be tapped open to reveal a porthole window that looks out over the rooftops and to the Tuscan hills beyond.

The information offered by Baciocchi oscillates between weighty and historical and vague. He is unlikely to engage in name-dropping, aside from the odd mention of Gio Ponti (regarding a vanity table with quintessentially splayed legs) or Angelo Mangiarotti (a hefty marble table). This isn't from modesty, but largely out of lack of interest. "I don't give a damn about who designed something," he declares. "I buy something solely because I like it." As we stand by what looks very much like an Arne Jacobsen chair, Baciocchi—ever the contrarian—admits to not liking Scandinavian furniture. "It's too, how shall I say, *predictable*."

Baciocchi prefers Italy's native treasures. In fact, an obsession with the richness of Italian culture permeates the home. In a long, hall-like room, for example, is a pristinely displayed collection of hundreds of cookbooks. Some 40 years in the making, its focus is almost entirely the cuisine of the Italian peninsula and its islands. Sleekly engraved magnetic steel plaques designate other miscellaneous subsections: Piedmont, Sardinia, Tuscany, "Flowers" and more.

"You know, I don't read stories or novels. I haven't read one since I was 18 years old," reveals the architect. "The fantasies of others do not interest me. I only read essays or histories." (And cookbooks, surely.) With its evolving chapters and unpredictable story lines, one wonders if this house is his novel? Baciocchi nods in approval. "Yes, indeed. I will allow that."

A different passion or avid curiosity manifests itself in each room, anteroom, hallway or chamber (none of the spaces have particular names, the architect insists). A love for craftsmanship is certainly clear, and Baciocchi has a phone book of dependable local artisans he can call on. Laid out on a work desk is a selection of objects that includes a prototype cutlery set. The hand-carved cherrywood handles are gnarled and the steel blades and forks are primitive and raw. Baciocchi holds a piece up, cherishing its rough beauty.

He holds even more affection for a collection of rather nondescript cast-iron objects that are stored by a giant stone fireplace in the kitchen—the inner sanctum of the house. Here, various spit-roast turners sit next to a vast quantity of cooking utensils and delicate Meissen porcelain. Perhaps conscious of being typecast as a hobbyist or a hoarder, Baciocchi says, "These are not *collections*. I use them all! And no, it's not *research*. I'm merely carrying something on here."

Baciocchi gives a tour of the lovely kitchen garden—a traditional Tuscan *orto* with carved stone benches and even a pretty little fresco that he excavated from soil and rubbish that had accumulated over the centuries. Now, small olive and fruit trees provide a canopy and there are immaculate rows of vegetables and herbs that grow despite the chill in the air. Ciro—the housekeeper who has been with the couple for two decades—cooks with the garden's fresh ingredients, using a beautifully designed scullery equipped with old granite worktops. "Oh no!" Baciocchi jokes. "This is where Ciro tries to poison us every night!"

Back upstairs, on the silvery gray velvet couch, Baciocchi ruminates more on his taste and how he approached filling his extraordinary house. Visual inspiration seems a deeply personal phenomenon, based on his respect for materials, function and origin. The house does not follow any design rules or preconceived ideas about comfort or luxury; every element—door knob, panel, step, nook, shelf—is a result of the 700-year history of the building, and Rosella and Roberto's thoughtful additions to it.

Baciocchi designs retail spaces, private residences, hotels and restaurants around the world. He is most celebrated for his work with Prada, La Perla and Miu Miu.

Baciocchi's meals often include produce from his own garden. A culinary enthusiast, Baciocchi has an extensive collection of cookbooks.

3
Relationships

Man's Best

For licking our friends and biting our enemies, we celebrate the endless loyalty of four-legged companions.

Friend

Photography by Elliott Erwitt

RELATIONSHIPS

RELATIONSHIPS

ISABEL

Words by Asher Ross, Photography by Christopher Ferguson & Styling by Debbie Hsieh

RUBEN

TOLEDO

To enter the loft of Isabel and Ruben Toledo is to ascend into a Borgesian sense of infinitude. Books, photographs, prints and mementos spill out of shelves and across tables. Vines and potted plants grow in the corners of a byzantine series of rooms that are at once a home and an atelier. The history of New York, in its most self-flattering mode, lives in countless objects: book collections gifted by Bill Cunningham, Klaus Nomi and other friends; a drafting table from the illustrator Antonio Lopez. Collectively, the objects would signify style and status were they not at the heart of the fairy tale embodied in Isabel and Ruben themselves. With an intensity that borders on obsession, their love for each other is the dominant presence in whichever room they inhabit and is the subtext of whatever idea they address. It's a love that shifts and reshapes itself constantly, making a harmony of their work, art and relationship. It has a constant presence, like the giant, ancient cactus that towers over one of the loft's larger rooms.

Isabel Toledo is a "designer's designer"; Narciso Rodriguez once called her his personal design hero. Over nearly four decades, her work has ranked among New York's uppermost fashion echelons and has constantly evolved, addressing shape, suspension and shadow in ways that have moved several critics to flights of poetry. In 2008, she reached that rarest of fashion milestones: crafting the inaugural dress for a first lady—Michelle Obama, no less. The most famous description of her work is "liquid architecture." The phrase conveys how her designs combine geometric and organic forms, and the way they toy with gravity.

Isabel was not yet ready for company when I arrived on a quiet, rainy morning. It fell to Ruben, the celebrated artist and fashion illustrator who is her husband and creative partner, to welcome me. He did so with an idiosyncratic blend of frank, New York enthusiasm and Cubano gentility. We would await the lady of the house together.

To pass the time, Ruben pulled out the catalog for his and Isabel's latest exhibition, *Bodies @ Work*, which features several of his large-scale paintings (shocking in size and abstraction, if you only knew Ruben for his whimsical fashion illustrations, which regularly appear in the pages of *Vogue*, *Harper's Bazaar* and *Elle*).

Noticing one of Isabel's works in the catalog—an antique sewing

Little of the decor in Isabel and Ruben's Manhattan home and studio is store-bought. Rather, the couple have made it themselves.

machine stitched top-to-bottom in black satin ("I dressed it," Isabel would later say)—Ruben brightened. "It's almost like a skinny animal. Quite beautiful." It was an introduction to two of Ruben's most essential qualities: an endlessly operative, strange imagination, and a fierce protectiveness of his wife's ideas. If you say something bland to Ruben, he'll gracefully make a joke; if you say something bland about Isabel's work, stand ready for correction.

Both Isabel's and Ruben's families fled Cuba as Castro consolidated power in the wake of the Cuban Revolution, arriving in the USA on the "freedom flights" of 1967 and 1968. Despite being uprooted so early in their lives, both share rich memories of their Cuban childhoods. Ruben was a city kid, born amid the chaos of the Bay of Pigs Invasion. The move to New York was not altogether shocking for him. "To me, this was totally natural—the multicultural thing, the craziness, the street life, the hustle and bustle. That's a normal Havana upbringing."

Isabel's origins were quite different. Born into a large family in the country town of Camajuaní, her earliest visual memories were suffused with a Caribbean light

that, as she puts it, "magnifies all silhouettes." She recalls her first exposure to geometric patterns in the hand-painted ceramic tiles that bordered her home's walls and floors. It was in this home that she began dissecting dolls and other objects, a deconstructive habit that would follow her through life. Most importantly, it was where she saw her first sewing machine.

If there is a creation myth to Isabel Toledo's style, it starts here. The sewing machine had belonged to her grandfather's first wife, a victim of tuberculosis whose ghost lent the object a sheen of mystery. "To me, it was a sculpture," Isabel says, "I played in it, even though I didn't know what the heck it was." She would spend hours beneath the machine, fascinated by its wrought-iron workings. But Isabel's Cuban childhood was not all charm. Her thin frame and fine-lined features (so unchanged when one looks at photos of her across the decades) felt unwelcome amid the voluptuousness of Cuban women.

"Growing up in a land very much in love with its endless curves," she wrote in her memoir, *Roots of Style*, "made my frail-looking, pointy body incredibly evi-

dent. As a child, I was weightless and sharp like a needle, and the 'shy' in me was born." This feeling would inform her later desire to create clothing that both protects the body and is structured enough to change its form.

The Toledos first met in high school in West New York, New Jersey. Ruben famously fell in love with Isabel at first sight, though it would take more than a decade for her to discover her own romantic feelings. In the meantime, the pair became immediate collaborators. Isabel, already making her own clothes, was fascinated by Ruben's drawings. They began traveling to the city at night along with other teenagers, plunging into Manhattan's nascent disco scene.

These nights have since become the stuff of New York lore. The Toledos witnessed the brass marching band that Steve Rubell and Ian Schrager hired for the opening night of Studio 54. They danced at Xenon and the Mudd Club. They immersed themselves in a heady scene made up of downtown artists, uptown whales, celebrities and bridge-and-tunnel kids—groups that are far more isolated in today's Manhattan.

Years later, they became close friends with *New York Times* fash-

"As a child, I was weightless and sharp like a needle, and the 'shy' in me was born."

Ruben's love of literature is evident in the couple's home. Not only does he collect books but he has inherited the libraries of close friends including illustrator Antonio Lopez, performer Klaus Nomi and fashion photographer Bill Cunningham. The result? "A library on every floor," says Ruben.

RELATIONSHIPS

Of his work dynamic with Isabel, Ruben says, "I want to see all of it happen, and that isn't practical. You can't end up with five different ideas. You have to narrow it down to one. And that's where I have to trust Isabel."

ion photographer Bill Cunningham. One night, he led them into his apartment at Carnegie Hall, revealing photographs he had taken of them as kids. The photos showed them piling into a car to head back to New Jersey; Isabel's daring, homemade dress had caught his eye. In typical Cunningham fashion, he had seen their love, and their talent, long before they knew about it themselves.

The Toledos got their first break on a class trip to the Museum of Modern Art. Lost in the rain, they stumbled into Fiorucci—the midtown shop presided over by the drag artist Joey Arias and known as the daytime Studio 54. Arias snatched Ruben's portfolio from under his arm, delighting in some hand-colored photographs of Isabel. He insisted that Ruben produce more, and began selling them as postcards.

At Fiorucci, the Toledos charmed (and were charmed in turn) by luminaries such as Klaus Nomi, Halston, Lena Horne and Andy Warhol, who would later feature them on his *Fifteen Minutes* television show. "Andy loved the exotic. He was curious about these Cuban teenagers," Ruben says.

The Toledos' path to success may seem gilded, but it was paved by relentless effort and ingenuity. Shortly after their marriage, for example, Ruben left their apartment with a small bundle of garments slung over his arm and returned with orders from Patricia Field, who ran an influential boutique on 8th Street, and Henri Bendel. They had a week to deliver the clothes, and almost no resources. They learned where to buy zippers and denim on the cheap. Ruben traced the outlines and Isabel stitched each garment by hand on a personal sewing machine. As she

In 2012, Isabel published a memoir, *Roots of Style*, recounting her journey as a designer and revealing the couple's philosophy on work, relationships and life more generally. Illustrations by Ruben can be found alongside Isabel's words throughout the book.

once wrote, "The only way to truly understand how every piece of [a] business can be assembled…is to do it all yourself."

Their improvisational spirit continued as the Toledo name spread through the city. They sent the invitations for their very first show in the form of hand-embroidered notes on white dress gloves (a flourish that caught the attention of *The New York Times*). They borrowed space from friends on 57th Street that would later become the headquarters for Louis Vuitton. The models, friends from Fiorucci, chose which dresses to wear themselves and did so in no particular order. The soundtrack was provided by a boom box in the middle of the room, and toward the end of the show the models had to kick it back to life when the batteries faded. The Toledos were a hit.

Following a cup of coffee, I ask Ruben if he misses the older, frothier New York. He says he still sees the old city behind the new, like a palimpsest. He refuses to be pigeonholed by nostalgia, but he admits a change. "All those different people in one room from such different polarities of life? That's unheard of now. Information has killed subculture to the point where everyone knows

about everything—nobody has the chance to fall in love with something. But I trust the kids. There's always something happening you don't know about … and don't let me know about it! Make it ferment so that it's such a beautiful stew by the time we meet it in culture."

Moments later, Ruben falls quiet and stands. Isabel is here. He introduces us and then excuses himself to get more coffee. I suppose that he wants to give me time to take in Isabel's presence on my own. This is likely out of pride, not politeness.

Both the Toledos want me to understand their love because they know it is essential to understanding their work. At the heart of their relationship is a very mysterious collaboration, one forged in those early days and perfected over time. With Ruben, this is a leitmotif as he glances from subject to subject. Isabel is far more direct.

"Did Ruben explain the theory of the vine as opposed to the tree?"

He had not.

"In a relationship, you should never be a tree, you should always be a vine. Trees grow, but they topple. Vines? Well, pieces fall off, but it keeps going."

Her voice is ardently, sensually serious. She gestures constantly

with her hands, not as a tick, but with a demonstrative choreography attending her words.

She gives her own account of Cuba, noting how its culture does not have the same generational divides that mark American society. She speaks about the early days in New York, pointing out, as a matter of clarification, that she had come to the city to dance on her own before Ruben ever accompanied her. She describes her love of sewing machines, of gardening, of taking things apart and putting them back together.

But when Ruben returns to the room, the conversation takes a permanent turn. The outer charm of the couple's love masks a deeper, tireless curiosity. They share an ability to communicate, often without words, in a way that retains the most fragile nuances of their vision.

So they begin, each following closely on the other's ideas. The themes constantly shift, like the thousand forms a dress can take as it moves across a street. They relate Isabel's darning to gender roles, to the feminine proclivity for the art of healing, to Isabel's passion for Betsy Ross, to the strange cardboard contraptions Ruben's father would create to protect avo-

cados and mangoes on his trips from New Jersey.

"You should see her darn socks! It's like a work of art! It's like braille!" Ruben says.

Isabel, discarding her previous line of thought for this newer, more exciting idea, does not miss a beat. "It's weaving. It's being able to put together again—a type of healing." Ruben continues: "The way she sews becomes like scarification. Whatever she was thinking at that moment is in the sock. You see it, you feel it."

Taking things apart is certainly Isabel's forte. During her internship under Diana Vreeland at the Metropolitan Museum of Art's Costume Institute, she immersed herself in dissection of classic couture—the work of legends like Madeleine Vionnet and Madame Grès, names to which critics would eventually resort to describe the potency of Isabel's own style.

The Toledos share a powerful sense of history, a conviction that fashion is not some march toward ever-greater sophistication, but a responsive, living cycle.

"Fashion is very modern in that way," Ruben says. "You can throw anything at it and it absorbs it. Nothing is repelled. It's an expert at vibrations and connections. That's why Isabel stopped doing shows. It's not a twice-yearly thing, it's a daily thing!"

"I would change five times a day, if I could," she notes. "And I do." This spirit is embodied in one of Ruben's most captivating drawings, a clockwork wheel surrounded by women in silhouette. The drawing happens to be printed on a scarf hanging near Ruben's table, and Isabel is delighted to rush over and discuss its nuances—how it reveals fascinating symmetries, and conveys the rule of echo, the reactive interweaving that lies at the root of the Toledo philosophy.

Once she has begun talking about her husband's work, it is difficult for her to stop. She pulls down one of hundreds of black notebooks, each filled to the brim with illustrations, ideas, forms in motion. They call these their "constant conversation." About Ruben's fashion illustrations, she

says, "You can get a room of women—all types, all nationalities—and they all see themselves in them. Women will always say, 'That's me to a T!'"

She calls Ruben her faucet, referring to the endless flow of his ideas, which she sees as her job to pare down. Her role is to pluck out what's best: "He's got to convince me, and the convincing part is quite interesting," she says. "It's like a courting," Ruben says, "You have to court each other to get there. You have to make them fall in love again."

Their collaborative mode is quite different when it comes to Isabel's work. She is not a draftswoman. Her process begins with fabric. She touches it, listens to it, senses how it wishes to fall and to fold, whether it wants to succumb to gravity or defy it. Once she understands the message, she calls out for Ruben, who is likely at work on his own project somewhere else in the loft.

"He's got to give an image to whatever I'm feeling and saying," she says. Ruben continues, "I have

to drop my ideas, I have to drop my stimulation, and just receive hers." This is not a demand most artists could tolerate.

It does not always work, and the Toledos are the first to laugh about it. Sometimes, for example, Isabel is forced to work with a mannequin. But more often it *does* work, and after a few moments Isabel sees her ideas appear beneath her husband's pencil. Their friend Kim Hastreiter, the founder of *Paper* magazine, once observed that Isabel's are "clothes for women who don't need men." But Isabel herself does need Ruben, just as he needs her. The clothes, the designs, the sets, the drawings come from a beautiful, very rare place between both of their minds.

For a couple whose image embodies sophistication, counter-culture and defiant style, there is something wonderfully traditional about their relationship. This contradiction seems of a piece with their Cuban-American identity. Theirs are hard-won convictions. They know what they know. And what they know, essentially, is love.

"In a relationship, you should never be a tree, you should always be a vine. Trees grow, but they topple. Vines? Well, pieces fall off, but it keeps going."

The Toledos tacitly communicate with and understand one another: If Isabel imagines a garment, she can tell her idea to Ruben who then translates her words into illustrations.

Yin

In the union of opposites, a delicate balance between tension and ease.

Photography by Zoltan Tombor & Styling by Debbie Hseih

Yang

Makeup: Linda Gradin, Hair: Fernando Torrent

Below: Ash wears a top by Beaufille and trousers by M. Martin. Right: Cheyenne wears a top by M. Martin.

Left: Cheyenne wears a top by Novis and trousers by Samuji. Below: Ash wears top and trousers by Céline and shoes by Tibi.

Below: Ash wears a dress by Barbara Casasola. Right: Cheyenne wears a top by Tibi, trousers by Colovos, coat by Jenni Kayne and shoes by Céline.

Relationships:

Trust
Intimacy
Independence
Communication

Words by Pip Usher & Photography by Zoltan Tombor

Trust

Sometimes ordinary life takes a turn for the worse. Like the totally average evening when your partner's phone bleeps with an incoming text message that throws your relationship off a cliff. Or a hurtful comment from a friend that snowballs into a savage severing of your shared history.

Cynthia Wall has a favorite way to describe the brutal shock of betrayal. Using an analogy borrowed from *The 7 Habits of Highly Effective People*, she describes trust as the oxygen in the room of relationships. When that vital life force is removed, the emotional pain can be visceral. "It's really the absence of trust that we feel," she says.

The author of *The Courage to Trust: A Guide to Building Deep and Lasting Relationships*, Wall has decades of experience as a therapist and social worker. We all, she points out, put superficial trust in others on a daily basis: the postal worker who stops by our house each morning, the driver in the car in front of us. But true trust springs from a willingness to share our inner selves—even when that exposure places us in a position of vulnerability.

"Our intimate relationships—and by intimate, I don't necessarily mean sexual—are those in which we can open up and say, 'This is who I am and how I'm really feeling,'" she says. "That's why intimate relationships are pretty total. They're literally, 'I'll reveal everything about myself, I'll show you this mole I hide from every-

one else, I'll tell you my deepest, darkest secret. Will you still love me then?'"

So what do you do when you've metaphorically—and perhaps literally—bared yourself to someone who then lets you down? Wall has been married for 36 years but admits her most brutal heartaches have been caused by friends who chose to end their friendship rather than confronting issues. In such situations, there's a lack of honesty; bad feelings are bottled up, situations silently escalate and no one dares break the ice until it completely freezes over. "Grinning and bearing it is acting like it's okay, but we need to say 'no'," she says. "To build trust is to say 'no' with kindness and compassion. And combining honesty with kindness builds trust. Or it wrecks the relationship," she adds. "But if a relationship cannot tolerate honesty when done well, then it doesn't have much legs to it."

Wall describes trust as a set of Russian nesting dolls: three layers, each stacked neatly inside the next. At the core is trust in oneself—the ability to count on yourself, stick to your word and to practice self-compassion when things go sideways. From there, it's necessary to develop trust in a positive future so that, even if a worst-case scenario plays out between you and a loved one, you feel confident knowing that hearing the truth is better than playacting a lie. With these components in place, it becomes possible to establish a rela-

tionship with someone else that is rooted in the risky, rewarding intimacy that comes from being willing to ask questions even when afraid of the answer.

"I wish I could have a watermark in my book saying, 'Everyone's afraid of rejection,'" says Wall with a gentle laugh. It's a sentiment worth keeping in mind when broaching a grievance; inherent in being the initiator of the discussion is that it immediately places the other person at a disadvantage. So, before starting a conversation, Wall recommends that you sit quietly and visualize how you would like it to go. Once you determine what you hope to achieve, put yourself in the other person's shoes. It helps to assume their actions were caused by obliviousness rather than any malicious intent. "What would she need to hear to know that she's hurt your feelings and that she needs to apologize without being made to feel like a bad person?" Wall asks. From there, pluck up the courage and ask to talk. Done well, it will bring new depths to your relationship.

"What might be a simple misunderstanding to one person could be a devastating reenactment of a betrayal to another person," says Wall. "And they're both right. It's about having the vulnerability to share those perspectives. If that's responded to with love and understanding as we clear up assumptions, then that makes a bond stronger than before."

Words by Pip Usher & Photography by Zoltan Tombor

Intimacy

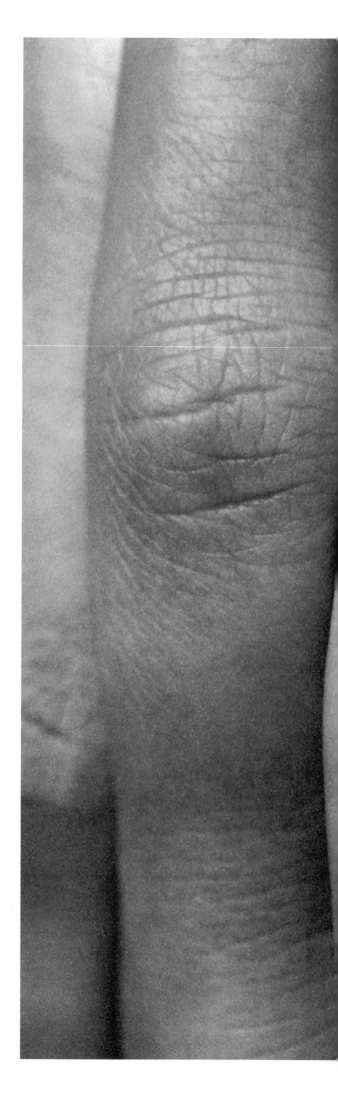

"Tantric sex is a way of having sex that invites a transformative, spiritual experience," says Barbara Carrellas, author of *Urban Tantra: Sacred Sex for the Twenty-First Century.* According to this centuries-old spiritual practice, the physical body is a manifestation of divine energy, which in turn means that sexual energy can be harnessed as a powerful tool in the journey toward enlightenment and intimacy. "It's not all about the sex," Barbara adds. "However, Tantric sex can be the door that opens into a Tantric life of mindfulness, connection and personal power."

Tantra encourages couples to focus solely on one another, without a rush toward the finish line. Many of its rituals transmute sex into something laced with far more profundity: eye contact, kissing, touch and synchronized breathing. Such techniques inspire a more intimate experience, which in turn fosters greater closeness and trust between partners. As Barbara explains, "Tantric sex invites participants to slow down, release expectations and goals, become more mindful, breathe more deeply and focus on the energetic aspects of sex—not just the physical. People become partners on a journey into the unknown with no

fixed agenda or anticipated result." Barbara suggests starting your own Tantric journey by researching the subject. Ten minutes of eye-gazing and slow breathing is a simple introductory exercise that couples can try together to deepen their intimate contact. But, she warns, the real work requires an overhaul of one's ingrained ideas about sex. In Tantra, there's less attention paid to "having" sex and more emphasis on encouraging erotic energy to flow through the body.

Barbara's own journey toward Tantra was driven by the AIDS epidemic in the 1980s. As she watched her community succumb physically and psychologically to the disease, she began to search for a sex-positive practice that would restore her strength. Tantra proved the perfect war cry, its message of spiritual growth and personal liberation correlating with an emphasis on cultivating sexual and political power. "Tantra is not couples therapy, nor is it exclusively for privileged, white, middle-aged, middle-class, apolitical, woo-woo, New Age workshop junkies," Barbara says firmly. All that's needed is a willingness to explore one's spirituality in its many guises, including the physical.

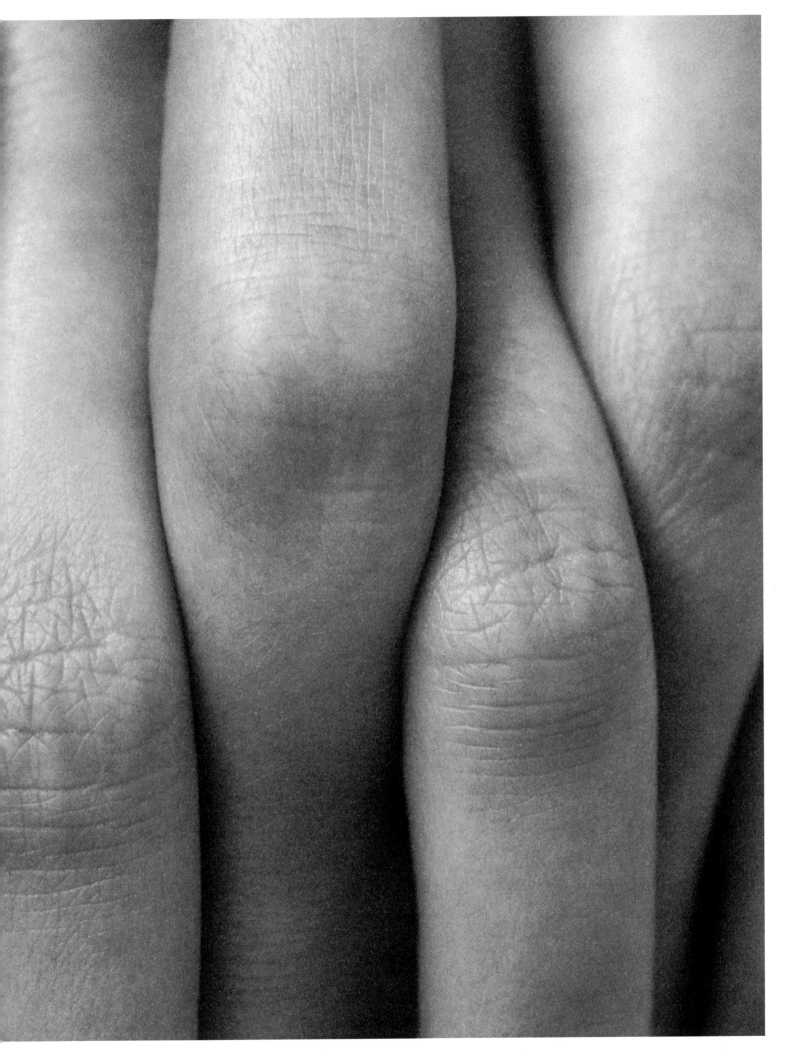

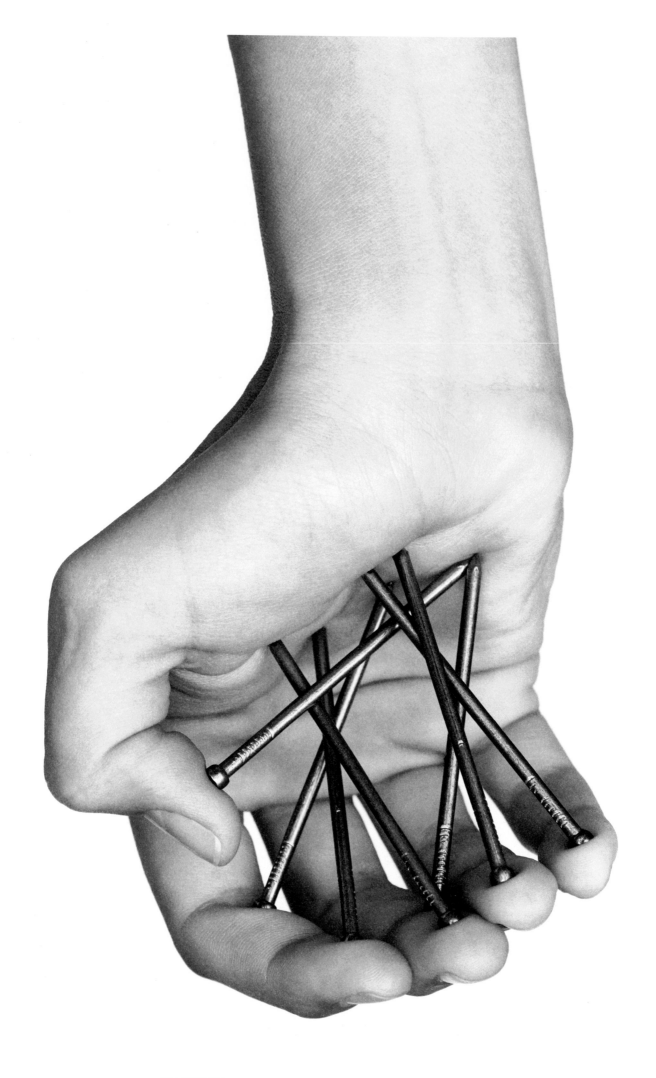

Words by Pip Usher & Photography by Zoltan Tombor

Independence

Striking just the right balance in relationships can be tricky: Absence either makes the heart grow fonder, or it causes the beloved to slip one's mind. In our relationships with others, the tightrope that spans romantic attachment and individual autonomy must be cautiously tread. Push too far in one direction and our identity is engulfed; hold back, and true intimacy evades us.

"Not being sucked into the relationship and drowned by it is so important," says Dr. Stephen Trudeau, a California-based clinical psychologist and the author of *Courage to Thrive: Triumph in the Face of Adversity*. Married for 21 years, Dr. Trudeau likes to tear around on his motorcycle—an obsession that has earned him the nickname "the Psych on the Bike"—while his wife prefers to attend '80s rock concerts with her girlfriends. The two have always been happy to let one another pursue individual interests in the belief that it strengthens them as a unit. "Because of our separate adventures, we have things to talk about, people to influence us, and other experiences that foster our continued growth as both separate people and as a couple," he says.

But for an independent relationship to work, there must be emotional infrastructure in place to support it. First, Dr. Trudeau emphasizes the necessity of open communication. Both parties should feel listened to and understood in moments of vulnerability. Second, he recommends adopting a two-way support system in which both partners take on the role of being the other's biggest cheerleader. Third, each person should selflessly keep their partner's best interests at heart. From that springs trust. With this trifecta in place, a supportive space emerges in which both people can explore their identities without losing common purpose as a couple.

A couple that allows for zero independence does so at their peril. Quash your differences and it's likely that you'll end up losing more than a hobby or two. What can start as an impassioned desire to please your partner and remain a deeply entrenched unit may result in a loss of respect from the very person you seek to please. "What attracts us to each other to begin with is the mystery of 'who is this person?'," says Dr. Trudeau. "If we let that go and let the relationship smother us, then we become unattractive to our partner."

The opposite end of the spectrum is no better, however, hence the tightrope walk. Independence should be fostered, but not at the cost of one's relationship. "Too much independence, and what value is the relationship?" says Dr. Trudeau. "When we couple up, we're saying, 'I want you in my life!'"

Words by Pip Usher & Photography by Zoltan Tombor

Communication

Dr. Gary Chapman has devoted decades to understanding why romantic relationships sour. The marriage counselor and pastor readily acknowledges that his own marriage was "miserable" in its early years. "My wife and I were in love, but we were missing each other, and our attempts to show love were falling short," he says. He noticed similar frustrations and hurt feelings erupting in the partnerships of those he counseled.

Determined to figure out why this disconnect was happening, Dr. Chapman began to sift through the years of notes he had accumulated during his professional life. As he catalogued his data, a pattern emerged; he published the results in his *New York Times* bestseller *The 5 Love Languages*, which has sold more than 11 million copies to date.

What Dr. Chapman's data had revealed was five distinct categories that explain how people communicate love: words of affirmation, acts of service, receiving gifts, quality time and physical touch. Couples ran into difficulty when they gave—and expected in return—a type of love that their partner didn't value as highly. That meant that a person raised in a household that prioritized acts of service—collecting one another's dry cleaning, cooking dinner—

could show their partner love on a daily basis, but such devotion may go unnoticed if the partner required the intimacy of physical touch or the thoughtfulness of a carefully selected gift instead. It wasn't that couples didn't love one another enough, Dr. Chapman discovered—it was simply that they didn't know how to communicate it in the way that would mean more to their partner. Once these communication preferences were revealed, couples were better equipped to make one another feel valued.

"I discovered that when a person began to speak the primary love language of their spouse or partner, the other person began to feel loved and the emotional climate of their relationship immediately began to improve," he says. "Learning to speak someone else's love language says to them that you are willing to do what it takes to communicate love and build a strong relationship," explains Dr. Chapman, whose own 50-year marriage improved after he had identified the love language concept. "That sometimes means learning to do what doesn't come naturally."

He points to the example of a newly married couple who successfully applied insight from *The 5 Love Languages* to the daily working of their relationship. The

wife had identified herself as an "acts of service" type, but she knew that her husband preferred words of affirmation—and so, during a routine email exchange, she decided to adopt his love language.

"My husband emailed me to let me know he was coming home from work. I wrote back, 'Great, I will start dinner,'" she recalled. "I immediately realized that was not in his style of communication, but in my preferred style. I did not receive an email back. So one minute later I wrote another email that said 'Love you. Can't wait to see you.' He immediately wrote back, 'You make me feel special.'"

Small adjustments, colossal impact. But Dr. Chapman warns that the work doesn't stop there. He suggests couples set a weekly date in which they sit down and address issues that are bringing conflict into their relationship. Checking in on a partner's emotional state—even if it brings up tricky truths about one's own faults and failures—will foster lasting intimacy.

"Ask them, 'How am I doing in my efforts to make you feel loved?'" he says. "This takes courage and a willingness to listen to their responses. But, if you're willing to ask each other these questions, you'll create an atmosphere of openness that will help to lessen reoccurring bad habits."

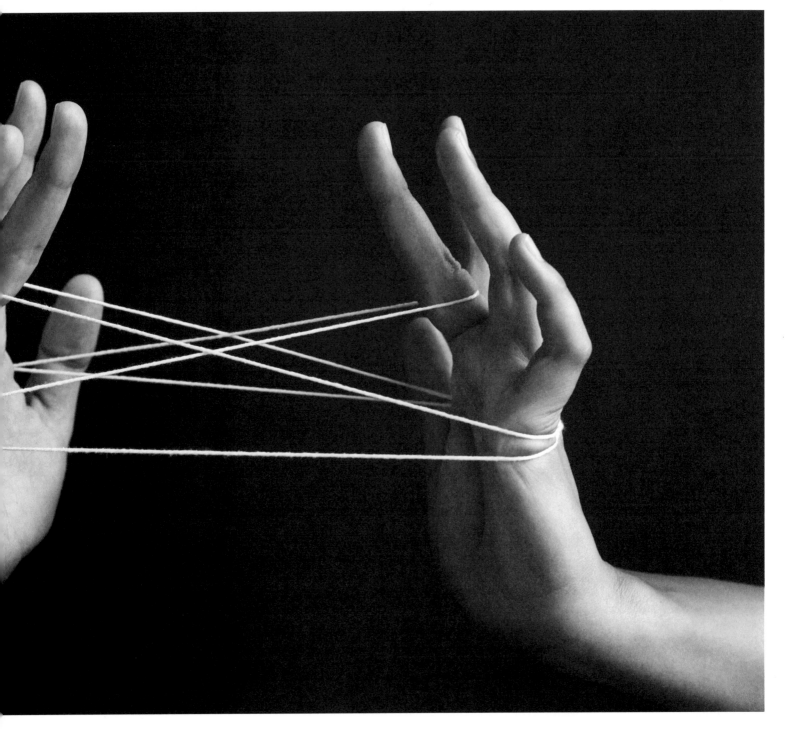

Why Do We Lie?

It is quite possible that we have never lied more. This has been a year of unpleasant new media coinages: "fake news," "post-truth," "alternative facts." In our private lives, technological advancement makes lying incrementally easier: Fibbing to a partner that you're "working late" slips out more easily screen-to-screen than face-to-face (although, even in person, 60 percent of us can't go 10 minutes without lying). Social media has accelerated the speed at which lies of all stripes are disseminated and then quickly debunked, and this cycle has most likely increased our own propensity to lie. According to the prominent American behavioral economist Dan Ariely, the more we are aware that dishonesty surrounds us, the more likely we are to spin falsehoods of our own.

And yet, we have never felt queasier about owning up to our own dishonesty. Paul Seager, psychologist and co-author of *Would I Lie to You?*, points to two polls conducted about lying, one from the early 1990s and one from the last decade. Between the two polls, he tells me, the number of people who claimed to *never* tell lies shot up from one in 12 to over one in three. When I ask Seager about the reason for the jump, he won't entertain the possibility that it is the result of a sudden flush of public piety. In fact, it's the opposite: "I think a lot more people lie than they used to," he says. "But I think people are very conscious about the way they paint themselves. We like to think we're living in a more enlightened society and there's no room for liars."

For philosophers and religious leaders, hand-wringing over the morality of lying is a well-established pursuit. For psychologists, it is not. As late as 1984, the only mention of lying in the hefty *Encyclopedia of Psychology* was a short entry on lie detection techniques. But over the last few decades, psychologists have entered the fray and their contribution has been a radical one, challenging our most basic presumptions about how honesty operates.

"Not lying is a cognitive impairment," says David Livingstone Smith, a professor of the philosophy of psychology at the University of New England, and part of a new wave of pragmatic—perhaps even amoral—logicians of deceit. "In order for society to function smoothly we have to keep ourselves in the dark, to a great extent."

For centuries, Livingstone Smith says, we have been obsessed with the idea of total honesty, a pursuit that has dampened the possibility of more nuanced discussions about how to distinguish good lies from bad. "There's been one current in philosophical thought about lying which I utterly reject—the idea that lying is always wrong," he says.

His main target here is the 18th-century German philosopher Immanuel Kant, a zealous moralizer so regular in his habits that, rumor has it, neighbors in Königsberg set their clocks by the time of his morning walk. Kant believed that the world should be governed by a set of unbending rules. These rules, he said, must be applicable to every situation and not adapted according to circumstance. Therefore, lying must always be wrong because society would collapse if there were a general rule that permitted dishonesty: "By a lie, a man throws away, and as it were, annihilates his dignity as a man," he insisted.

He was unbending in his application of the principle. What if an ax murderer came to the door demanding the whereabouts of your family so he could kill them? Let them in, Kant counseled, even tell them where your family is hiding. "Truthfulness," he wrote, "is the formal duty of man to everyone, however great the disadvantage that may arise therefrom for him or for any other."

Kant's absolutism is jarring in its extremes, and yet he remains perhaps the most important moral theorist of modernity—a touchstone not just for philosophers but also literary figures from Coleridge to Goethe (the latter compared discovering his moral counsel to "walking into a lighted room").

Others argue that we must reach back further to identify the root of our moral absolutism. Dallas Denery, chair of the history department at Bowdoin College, says that he thinks Western societies' discomfort with dishonesty stems from the confusing and often contradictory ways that lying is framed in the Bible.

Denery, who first became interested in deceit when his mother made him watch the three-week-long Watergate trial on television in 1973, begins his 2015 book, *The Devil Wins*, in the Garden of Eden, at the moment when Eve is

When we lie, shame and chagrin can befall not only ourselves but also those we deceive. Philosophers, however, argue that there exists a socially endorsed form of dishonesty, and that lying might even be what keeps the world turning. To help make sense of lying in an age in which trumped-up stories now infiltrate our news channels, politics and daily reality more than ever before, *Harriet Fitch Little* examines the difference between telling a "good lie" and being a good liar.

deciding whether to pluck the apple that God has forbidden her from eating. "You shall not surely die," the serpent cajoles her, convincing her to bite into the fruit. This, Denery says, is the first lie, and its consequences are catastrophic: Man is banished from paradise, learns to feel shame and sin, and becomes mortal.

"Lying was always the seminal event that frames our connection to the world we live in," he explains. "So any discussion of lying has this resonance that it is what undid the world—it is what makes the world so terrible."

Denery's argument goes beyond scriptural analysis. Much of *The Devil Wins* is given over to discussing the strange shapes that the pious have contorted themselves into over the centuries to avoid lying.

Often, Denery says, the solution has been word games—linguistic tricks that allow devout priests and laymen to conceal the truth without overtly lying. Making sentences grammatically ambiguous is one option. For example, in response to Kant's ax murderer requesting the whereabouts of your family, you might in good conscience respond: "They're not here," by which you mean, privately, that they are not standing on the exact same spot that you are.

The technique of mental reservation involved a similar sleight of tongue. Originally coined by the Basque theologian Martín de Azpilcueta, it suggested that one might start a sentence out loud with a lie, but add something to the end of it in your head that made it

truthful. So, to take a contemporary example, when Bill Clinton infamously declared "I did not have sexual relations with that woman," he might have perhaps salved his conscience by adding under his breath, "...in a way that is any of your business."

"Mental reservation is probably up there with my favorites in terms of how you justify this sort of behavior," says Denery, laughing. "The idea is that you're talking to God so, when you finish statements in your head, God is listening anyway and knows you told Him the truth." I ask Denery if he has ever come across a convincing moral system built on a categorical refusal to lie. "No!" he says. "No one does that. In part because the Bible, where people look to guide their decisions, is in itself full of deceptions."

Denery's work charts a gradual evolution of the way lying is viewed by society. For a long time, deceit was seen as a manifestation of the devil and liars were treated as possessed. Ancient techniques for detecting falsehood included trial by submersion in water, which relied on the idea that because the devil hated water, those possessed by his spirit would quickly bounce back up to the surface (the innocent, unfortunately, would sink).

Gradually, Denery says, the way we viewed lies shifted: Rather than seeing them as a devilish device, they became a social one. "People start thinking, 'Wow—sometimes I do need to lie to survive, to accomplish important tasks'," he explains. "Over time this thinking began to

snowball. So it went from the vision of lying as the thing that caused everything to go wrong, to lying as the thing that binds us all together."

This acceptance of lying as useful within reason is the current orthodoxy: We know we may lie so as not to hurt others' feelings, so we can express our creativity through storytelling, to maintain our privacy against prying eyes, and to simplify emotions too complex to put into words. We recognize that those who struggle to lie effectively—young children, or some people on the autism spectrum—are not being virtuous, but are cognitively incapable of lying.

But when contemporary psychologists describe total honesty as impossible, they are hinting at something far more radical. Lying, says Livingstone Smith, is not simply a social lubricant, but a behavior so deeply entrenched in our biology that we are often totally unaware of where it ends or begins. As he puts it: "We spend our lives being duped by our own minds."

This argument is an evolutionary one. The brain, Livingstone Smith says, has evolved like all other organs to contribute to our reproductive success. To do so, it is often beneficial for us to deceive ourselves. In his 2004 book, *Why We Lie*, he eases readers into this notion by citing examples from the animal kingdom that we would not automatically recognize as deception: the way insects camouflage themselves against trees, the octopi who create fake outlines of their bodies by squirting ink to mislead predators, the male snakes who pretend to be female so that a huddle will form around them and raise their body temperature after hibernation.

Livingstone Smith says that we are often no more conscious of our lies than cross-dressing snakes are of theirs. To make his point, he reels off studies that demonstrate how wrong our views about ourselves often are, among them the fact that 93 percent of drivers deem themselves better than average, 25 percent of people rate themselves in the top one percent in terms of their ability to get along with others and—in one headline-grabbing experiment—that homophobic men become more aroused by gay pornography than non-homophobic heterosexual men. The conclusion he draws from these disparate examples is simple: "In hiding the truth from ourselves, we are able to hide it more fully from others."

Livingstone Smith's argument—compelling as it is—is tarred to a certain extent by his disciplinary leanings. He is an evolutionary biologist and heavily influenced by Freudian psychology, two schools of thought that find little favor within the empirically driven scientific community. But he is far from alone in making the case that lying is often something we have little control over.

In his 2012 book, *The (Honest) Truth About Dishonesty*, Dan Ariely presents an evidence-based case very similar to Livingstone Smith's theory that highlights our distinct inability to separate truth from lies even in our own actions. Not only do we lie (and frequently), says Ariely, but we also appear staggeringly predisposed to believe our own falsehoods.

Ariely's favorite device is to give his test subjects an exam in which they have the ability to cheat by checking the answers, a set-up which he then adjusts for different variables that might increase or decrease the decision to be dishonest. The strangest and most compelling iteration of the test that Ariely records in

his book concerns a pair of designer sunglasses. In it, the author gives a group of women Chloé sunglasses to wear, telling some that the glasses are real and others that they are fake. After a few time-wasting exercises he then has the women complete one of his cheatable tests. The results showed a striking divide: While 30 percent of women who believed they really were wearing designer eyewear cheated, a staggering 74 percent of those wearing the supposedly fake glasses did. Furthermore, when they later completed a survey on general attitudes, the subjects who had been wearing fake designer glasses were far more likely than the norm to see the general population as dishonest and likely to cheat them in business dealings. Ariely's conclusion, in this and his other tests, is that we have far less control over our decision to lie than we might generally imagine.

There is something disconcerting about this dissolving of barriers between truth and fiction. And yet, the evidence would suggest that our ability to lie to ourselves is, in fact, supremely useful. In the same way that lies are necessary for society's smooth running, they are also necessary for our own mental health. The most compelling evidence for this comes from studies of people suffering from depression, who are far less likely than non-depressed individuals to delude themselves about the extent of their own abilities, or the level of control they have over a particular situation.

If we pause to reflect on this, examples of the fact that lies can be sustaining are to be found everywhere. In Arthur Miller's *Death of a Salesman*, the aging Willy is buoyed by imagining himself as illustrious and influential, and commits suicide when that illusion is shattered. In comedian Ricky Gervais' otherwise anodyne 2009 rom-com, *The Invention of Lying*—a film set in a world in which nobody lies—the only poignant moment comes when Gervais' character informs his dying mother

"Evidence suggests that our ability to lie to ourselves is, in fact, supremely useful. In the same way that lies are necessary for society's smooth running, they are also necessary for our own mental health."

that heaven is waiting for her and that death will not be painful. He has invented the world's first compassionate lie, and the old woman slips away with a smile on her face. Indeed, Ariely himself is aware of the sustaining power of deceit through drastic personal circumstances: As a teenager he suffered third-degree burns over 70 percent of his body, and says that it was only because the nurses allowed him to believe that removing his bandages wouldn't be painful that he felt able to go through with the treatment.

This is a new and still controversial field of inquiry: Psychology has, as a discipline, built itself on the idea that the mind is a knowable and rational entity whose default setting is truthfulness. In this telling of it, lies are a perversion of our "default" setting, and therefore should be identifiable—if only we can find the right code to do so.

Melissa Littlefield, author of *The Lying Brain*, tells me that there are few places where this conflict is more evident than in the lucrative field of lie detection—a discipline that is, she says, "based on the belief that it's possible to isolate what lying is."

Littlefield rattles off a list of the various methods that have been used to detect lies over the centuries: rice chewing, hot blades on tongues, polygraph tests and—most recently—brain imaging techniques. Every technique, she says, relies on the same assumption: Lies must somehow manifest themselves physically. In the case of rice and hot blades, saliva was believed to be the giveaway—it was reasoned that the guilty would be nervous and their mouths would go dry, so the rice would not be masticated, the blade would burn the tongue. In the 20th century, the polygraph test replaced these crude measures with slightly more subtle iterations: readings of blood pressure, pulse, respiration and skin conductivity. Recently, scientists have developed techniques of brain

imaging which they claim are able to detect the presence of lies in the central nervous system.

Littlefield is skeptical. She says that regardless of how sophisticated the tests are getting, they rely on an identical belief that lies can be extracted from the body in a meaningful way. "We're completely dedicated to the idea of a machine," she says. "We keep changing what the machine actually is, what it measures. We keep on saying, 'Oh no—*this* is the thing we can't control, so *that's* where we'll find the truth…' but that's the same narrative we keep coming back to. It's pervasive."

Littlefield points out that this faith in technological solutions is particularly ironic given that many pioneers of lie detection were sharply attuned to the fact that lying was often an unconscious activity. Polygraph inventor William Moulton Marston (also the creator of *Wonder Woman*) built his public brand in the 1930s on conducting bombastic tests that aimed to show how his lie detector could root out emotions of which even the test taker was unaware. In one partnership with shaving brand Gillette, he used his polygraph to demonstrate that men felt significantly more stressed when using non-Gillette razors to shave—even if they professed that they weren't aware of the difference. "He was totally obsessed with people who are self-deceivers," says Littlefield. "And he believed the lie detector could actually help—at least that was the way he presented it in the media."

When I ask Littlefield whether she personally thinks that a world without lies could ever be possible, her answer comes from an unusual place: science fiction. She cites two popular books that project utopian visions of worlds without lies—Alfred Bester's *The Demolished Man* from 1953, and James L. Halperin's *The Truth Machine* from 1996. In both, she explains, the author imagines a world where some method of lie detection has made deception all but

impossible and in both cases, the results are beyond rapturous: Crime disappears, education and even life span see a dramatic boost.

But, Littlefield tells me, both books have at their center a protagonist who *is* capable of lying—a God-like figure who stands outside the purview of the lie detection. Why? "Because it just doesn't work without it," she insists. "It's like how you can't know light without darkness. Without having the one person who can lie, the system can't function because it's this impossible, imaginary thing." Lies, it seems, always find a way to sneak in—even to utopias.

Perhaps the reason that we find this discussion so disconcerting is because, as Littlefield's history of lie detectors demonstrates, we have proven to be uncannily bad at separating fact from fiction. Lie detection techniques are still unreliable, and without any technology at our disposal we are on average able to tell when someone is lying 53 percent of the time—only infinitesimally better than guesswork. Even police and law enforcement officers can't beat this average. In fact, we are so bad at rooting out lies that an evolutionary psychologist might be inclined to suggest that there is something intentional about this blind spot: For society to function smoothly, there are certain things that we are better off not knowing.

These are conversation topics that prompt heated emotions, and rightly so: That we are becoming increasingly aware of the importance of lies does not displace the fact that, without honesty as our basic modus operandi, human interactions and even the logic of language would collapse entirely. But we should at least be cautiously appreciative of the mysterious creativity, freedom and ability to refashion ourselves in new ways that lying to ourselves and to others sometimes affords us. As Livingstone Smith puts it, "The mind is not a fishbowl." We are richer for it.

Language

A wordless tongue, understood around the world.

# of Flowers

Words by Asher Ross, Arrangements by Marisa Competello & Photography by Zoltan Tombor

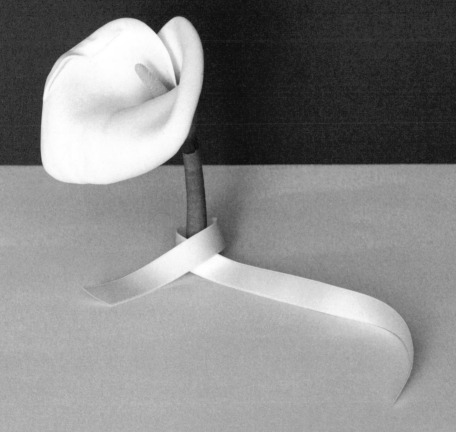

The corsage, brought nervously by teenagers to doorsteps every year, is a talisman of purity given on a mission of desire. The name derives from the French word for the bodice of a dress, where flowers were pinned on formal occasions. One gives a corsage in full sight of someone's family. It signifies a promise to protect while hinting at more passionate motives. The calla is a flower with similarly parallel meanings. It has a long association with purity, even with the Virgin Mary. Yet in its unfurling there is unmistakable sexuality, a fact not lost on two of its most famous admirers, Sigmund Freud and Georgia O'Keeffe.

We rely on flowers, like music, to express emotions that seem too raw, sacred or risqué for words. There is no lingua franca in the floral world; a lily would mean something quite different to a lady of the Tang court and a high-toned matron of Boston. Flowers accumulate meanings and then let them fall away. Take the rose. For Dante, it symbolized the multifoliate arrangement of divine love in heaven, yet for Gertrude Stein ("a rose is a rose is a rose") it was proof of plain being. George Orwell, railing at the decay of his beloved English language, decried the growing preference for scientific flower names (chrysanthemum, say) over the older, more descriptive forget-me-nots and snapdragons.

Buddha found Nirvana atop a lotus bloom, and the ancient Norse believed the worlds were interwoven in the branches of Yggdrasil, the world tree. In the modern West, obsession with a complex and blush-worthy language of flowers reached its zenith during the 19th century. Though most of us can no longer read the difference between melancholic longing and burning passion in a bouquet, certain events still send even the least poetic among us to the florist: birth, love and death. Perhaps it's time to revive a subtler language of flowers, one that serves the quieter milestones of our emotional lives.

Set Design by Sam Jaspersohn

Ceremony

Ceremonies, whether somber or wild, divine or secular, seek to temporarily elevate human action to a higher realm. In ancient Greece, the laurel wreath gave fleeting divinity to triumphant poets and athletes, and the *thyrsus*, a plant-spear topped with a pinecone, was hoisted amid the ecstatic revels of the Dionysian cult. A crown of flowers was given to high-born women during medieval festivals, raising them to a presiding role atop the hierarchy of courtly love. On the Día de Muertos, Mexicans haul out marigolds by the millions to welcome the returning dead. Cherry blossoms draw Japanese to the *Hanami*, a countrywide meditation on transience. And the image of a single cherry blossom adorned the hulls of planes used on suicide missions by Japanese pilots in World War II. This simple arrangement of budding quince and heliconia speaks of a quieter, more peaceful ceremony. Also known as the "false bird of paradise," the heliconia gives a glimpse of another world. The upright blooms of the quince show the promise of early spring and its sweet ceremony of renewal.

We give flowers to the people we desire. It's a way of saying "something has grown inside me, about you." Flower-giving is a pan-cultural element of courtship and seduction, a metaphor that few can resist. The world's poets, however, have long worried over the fact that these symbolic flowers have a habit of withering. Here we see love in crimson and black. The fruit-bearing Anthurium, or "tail-feather," encloses male and female structures within each of its blooms, testifying to love without distinction of gender. It bares all—seducing with naked, blood-red biology. The Anthurium is a flower from the Americas, and is free of old-world associations. It is unfamiliar and undisguised, as new love should be.

Housewarming

The housewarming ritual has two aims: to get on good terms with the spirits of a place and to ensure a safe and nourishing refuge. Romans would build shrines to their household deities, or lares, while medieval Europeans used bread and salt to bless a new home. Hindu culture includes the performance of Griha Pravesh, a purification ceremony in which husband and wife heft a copper pot into the house, and cause it to boil over with sweetened milk. Greeks like to give pomegranates at housewarming parties. Here we see other vegetables and fruits that convey strength, plentitude and durability. The armored artichoke, the earthy rutabaga, the parsnip that grows sweeter despite winter frosts. The dragon fruit (like those Greek pomegranates) hides fertility beneath its tough exterior: strong walls protect love and growth. Yet a home needs beauty also. The musa, or banana flower, gives fruit and ornament in equal measure.

In the ancient world, the beloved dead were celebrated with both feasts and somber rites. Funeral games—athletic competitions held in honor of the deceased—interrupted action in both *The Iliad* and *The Aeneid.* Gifts were often sent down with the dead to aid them in the afterlife, a tradition that reached its apex in the elaborate preparations undertaken for the pharaohs. Not all have forgotten how to embrace death with gusto. Blending traditions from Africa, the Caribbean and Europe, the citizens of New Orleans hold jazz marches at funerals. The music is somber until the crowd "cuts the body loose," exchanging grief for joy as the soul is freed to God. The Amaranthus, from the Greek word for unfading, has long signified respect for the dead, and hope for their immortality. Its grain was an Aztec staple and is still used to make sugar skulls on the Día de Muertos. The flower was said to grow next to the tree of life in paradise. And it was worn by mourners at the funeral of Achilles. For us mortals, this overflowing bowl of amaranth signifies the bounty of memory—and our refusal to let it fade.

Lei

Leis are a floral language unto themselves. The choice of flower and arrangement can signify a new beginning or the accomplishment of a difficult task. Love, marriage, mourning, birth, graduation, New Year—there is a lei, it seems, for each emotion, each event. Tourists expect a kiss when they are given one, but older tradition dictates the exchange of *ha*, or "breath," a gesture in which both people exhale and inhale, cheek-to-cheek, transmitting the part of themselves that cannot be put into words. Leis are meant to be cherished. They signify the loving patience of the hands that gathered the flowers and worked all afternoon to string them. You infuse your feelings while making a lei, and you give part of yourself along with it. Less fragrant varieties, like this cigar lei, are usually reserved for men. The name comes from the way the autumnal reds, oranges and yellows of the kika flower resemble a cigar in various stages of combustion.

4
Directory

JESSICA LYNNE

James Baldwin

Few authors have shaped political and cultural discourse as elegantly or unflinchingly as James Baldwin. Against the backdrop of the civil rights movement, he emerged in the '60s as a searing critic of the conditions of black people in the United States. Jim Crow laws in the South dictated terms of segregation; the epidemics of lynching and state-sanctioned violence terrorized black communities throughout the region. And as black families migrated to northern cities in hopes of reaching equity and justice, they were met with a host of de facto policies that limited access to secure housing, jobs and full livelihoods.

"The American soil is full of corpses of my ancestors, through 400 years and at least three wars," Baldwin asserted during a 1965 debate against William F. Buckley Jr. at Cambridge University. "Why is my freedom, my citizenship, in question now? What one begs American people to do, for all sakes, is simply to accept our history." His writings were indictments of a political system that had consistently rendered black Americans second-class citizens.

It was his first collection of essays, *Notes of A Native Son*, published in 1955, that truly ushered Baldwin into national prominence. The collection traversed the realms of literary criticism, political theory and memoir, as Baldwin addressed the consequences of racism in a country

he regarded as existing in severe moral decay. In "Everybody's Protest Novel," Baldwin casts Bigger Thomas, the central protagonist of Richard Wright's acclaimed novel *Native Son*, as nothing more than a caricature of an angry black man. In "Encounter on the Seine," Baldwin recounts his interactions with Africans living in France and presents a poignant comparison to the ways in which blackness operates in France, Baldwin's longtime home, and the United States, his birthplace. What permeates this first collection is a biographical inquiry rooted in a critical analysis of race, a reconciliation to which he returns repeatedly.

James Arthur Baldwin was born in 1924 in Harlem, New York, and came of age in a neighborhood that teemed with an "...insistent, maddening, claustrophobic pounding in the skull that comes from trying to breathe in a room with all the windows shut," as he described in the essay "The Harlem Ghetto." Baldwin considered the conditions of Harlem to be the direct result of the material consequences of institutionalized racism: housing discrimination, lack of jobs, poverty. Baldwin's home life was largely informed by the influence of his stepfather, a preacher, with whom he had a tenuous relationship. In fact, for a short while, Baldwin himself was a preacher. But, it was the classroom that offered the greatest solace, and it was as a student that Baldwin began to nurture and devel-

op his love of writing. By the time his stepfather died in 1943, the 19-year-old Baldwin had committed fully to the pursuit of writing, leaving Harlem for Greenwich Village. It was there he met fellow author Richard Wright and painter Beauford Delaney, who served as guides for a young Baldwin navigating the downtown scene.

Despite being embraced by a community of like minds, Baldwin was disillusioned by the pervasiveness of prejudice in the United States. And so he left for Paris in 1948, arriving in the city with just $40 in his pocket. Baldwin's departure from his homeland was, quite literally, a matter of life and death. In a 1984 interview with Jordan Elgrably of *The Paris Review*, he put it this way: "My luck was running out. I was going to go to jail, I was going to kill somebody or be killed. My best friend had committed suicide two years earlier, jumping off the George Washington Bridge." Later in the interview, he is even more explicit: "It wasn't so much a matter of choosing France—it was a matter of getting out of America. I didn't know what was going to happen to me in France but I knew what was going to happen to me in New York. If I had stayed there, I would have gone under, like my friend on the George Washington Bridge."

In France, Baldwin joined a growing cohort of black American expat artists who viewed their self-exile as a means of escaping the physical and psychological

trappings of a country that refused to recognize the fullness of their humanity. He spent time in Switzerland and Turkey before returning to the US in 1957, but his transatlantic reckoning never formally ended. France remained a haven throughout his life.

Once back in the US, Baldwin became deeply embedded in the civil rights movement, traveling throughout the South to cities such as Birmingham, Alabama and Jackson, Mississippi to chronicle the injustices of codified disenfranchisement. He befriended and supported leaders like Malcolm X and Rev. Dr. Martin Luther King Jr., and found himself heralded as a voice equally as urgent as theirs in the midst of a black liberation struggle. "It is entirely unacceptable that I should have no voice in the political affairs of my own country," he writes in his seminal nonfiction work, *The Fire Next Time*, "for I am not a ward of America; I am one of the first Americans to arrive on these shores."

Indeed, unrelenting in his love for his people, unyielding in his commitment to justice, Baldwin used his pen as a tool for truth-telling, producing more than 18 works of nonfiction, fiction, poetry and screenplays. He never saw himself as a revolutionary leader. Instead, he thought of himself, as he once told filmmaker Sedat Pakay, as a witness; there was potency in his looking, his observations and his proclamations.

In 1970, James Baldwin returned to France and purchased a farmhouse in the southern town of Saint-Paul-de-Vence where he remained for the final 17 years of his life. He is pictured in the Provençal home here.

Letter writing, the endangered species of correspondence, is responsible for nurturing some of history's most celebrated relationships. Thankfully, it has also documented them.

ALEX ANDERSON

Relationships in Letters

Most of our written correspondence happens quickly, urgently. A few words appear; we respond; they disappear. Sometimes, though, a real letter arrives, and that invites attention and time. Personal, handwritten correspondence, so common only a generation ago, has now become unexpected, and, while not quite a lost art, it is rare enough to provoke some examination.

To begin, consider the letter as defined five centuries ago by Flemish philologist Justus Lipsius in *Principles of Letter-Writing*. "A letter," he says, is "a message of the mind to someone who is absent." Letters travel over distance and time to bind people together. And, with their very physical presence, they convey thoughts, feelings and emotions in ways not possible using other means.

Subtle cues in structure and language control expression in handwritten letters. Because a letter is composed rather than extemporized, it shapes statements more deliberately than conversation. And the flow of the pen can hint at passion, authority, reserve, desperation—encoding more than words can offer. A letter thereby exceeds its explicit message; it communicates, as Lipsius suggests, some crucial unstated intention of the mind. Each part of the letter—date, address, salutation, body, closure, signature and postscript—carries its own encrypted information, its own unstated message. A recipient's address placed before the salutation reveals that this is a formal rather than an emotional transaction. With which prefatory term (My Dearest, Dear, Hi) does the greeting begin? Or does it start more abruptly—even rudely—with just a name? Is there a comma or colon after? The latter is the more assertive. But even before a letter is composed, the material upon which it is written will carry implications. Greeks sent notes to associates and friends (and curses against enemies) inscribed on reusable sheets of lead. Roman soldiers stationed in the hinterlands communicated on thin tablets of birch, alder or oak—whatever was available—using ink made with carbon black. Histiaeus of Miletus sent a secret letter to collaborators in Persia tattooed on the scalp of a messenger. Later, letters usually traveled on parchment of stretched sheepskin or calfskin. The missives with which we are most familiar, though, arrive on paper.

Occasionally, a letter appears among catalogs and bills, hand addressed and on fine paper (its rarity these days making it all the more notable). The elegant penmanship delights the eye; the texture of paper greets the fingers; the seal enforces anticipation.

As the sender has folded the letter, so do we unfold it, and our hands are connected over distance. The deliberate decoding of handwriting, spacing, salutation and closure slows the pace of reading. And whether it carries sorrow or joy, a physical letter sustains bonds as no other kind of communication can.

Letters sooth yearning, assuage loss, resolve anxiety, convey affection or negotiate difference; they inform, advise, warn. They bridge the gaps that distance enforces—whether across the world or just across town. We see vividly in them—in their material substance and rich idiosyncrasies of penmanship and structure—how deliberate communication through letters can maintain powerful connections of the mind and heart across absence.

O'KEEFFE TO STIEGLITZ, 1943

Alfred
I feel so sick over going away from you that it is very very hard for me to move. It makes nothing that I can imagine ahead seem good—I only remember that I liked it there before—
Yes—it makes me feel very—very sick
I guess I am really fond of you
A good night good night kiss to you.
Be very good to your self—

Over their long friendship, love and marriage Georgia O'Keeffe and Alfred Stieglitz produced more than 25,000 pages of handwritten letters. O'Keeffe left this short, anguished note on a table in their New York home before she left for New Mexico, where she lived and painted each summer. They often spent long periods apart, and wrote to each other almost daily during those times in a detailed, cross-country correspondence. When she wrote this in 1943, they had been together for nearly 35 years, and their affection and comfort with each other, their need for each other, is palpable. It's a quick note, probably written as she prepared to leave their darkened home to catch a late train. We can almost imagine the luggage waiting by the door. A companion note showed up in the morning, tucked under Stieglitz's pillow with "a good night pat and kiss." A third note appeared in a robe pocket, and advised in the same green ink:

Good Night
a day
Take two pills please!

Good night—

O'Keeffe sent a telegram from Santa Fe two days later to let Stieglitz know she had arrived, and toward the end of their first week apart wondered in a letter whether he was taking two pills a day. Although her handwriting is always exuberant, O'Keeffe's unsettling departure seems to have checked her pen somewhat in this letter.

Alfred — I feel so sick over going away from
you that it's very very hard for me to move.
It makes nothing that I can imagine ahea
seem good — I only remember that I liked it
here before ~

Yes ~ it makes me feel very ~

very sick

I guess I am really fond of you

A good night good night dear dear

Be very good ~ I love you dear self ~

CHARLES SHAFAIEH

Cooling-Off Periods

Though still invaluable on a sweltering day, the handheld fan was once a much more common item. Employed in religious ceremonies, dances and as an accessory in the act of mourning, it had a ubiquitous presence throughout history from Mesoamerica to North Africa and Europe. Believed to have helped stoke flames during humankind's earliest days, the handheld fan appears in ancient Egyptian hieroglyphics dating from as early as 3000 B.C. In many of its earliest known representations, the fan was shown as an accoutrement of the wealthy and powerful. A preserved seven-inch fan made of carved ivory and feathers was recovered from King Tutankhamen's tomb, while fans mounted on poles and held by attendants were used to cool and provide shade for pharaohs. Euripides, in his play *Orestes*, also writes about a eunuch using a fan to shield Menelaus from sun and other creaturely disturbances. A similar need would be fulfilled centuries later in the Roman Catholic Church by a peacock-feathered version called a flabellum.

Whether feathered or made of sturdier material, handheld fans were fixed in shape and structure. The folding variety, with its delicate, accordion body, can be traced back to ninth-century Japan. This design—which scholars believe was created to resemble the wings of a bat—replaced its more rigid European predecessor by the end of the 17th century and increased the object's fashionability. Around this time, too, fan production spread outward from its hub in France. Louis XIV's revocation of the Edict of Nantes in 1685 prompted a mass exodus of French Protestants, many of whom were skilled artisanal craftsmen, to England and other nearby countries, taking their fan-making knowledge with them.

Unlike the cockade fan, which never quite caught on—likely because its 360-degree spread made it difficult to handle—the folding fan and its approximately 170-degree surface was a beloved canvas for artists. Mother-of-pearl, gold, silk, lace and lacquer were used in the most richly designed examples, some of which were illustrated with pastoral scenes from Greco-Roman mythology. Others featured the work of renowned impressionist painters.

Handheld fans also served a semiotic function. The French writer Madame de Staël once commented, "What graces does not a fan place at a woman's disposal if she only knows how to use it properly. I will wager that in all the paraphernalia of the loveliest and best-dressed women in the world, there is no ornament with which she can produce so great an effect."

In China, the Cultural Revolution virtually destroyed the country's long history of producing artisanal items, including fans (those that were made subsequently were constructed in factories and often featured pro-Mao symbolism). Fans are, however, still widely found in Japan.

The *gunsen*, or war fan, is no longer needed as a signaling instrument, but other types remain important facets of sumo wrestling, the martial art *tessenjutsu*, and Noh and Kabuki theaters. Often used during the formal tea ceremony, the *rikiu ogi*, invented in the 16th century, is used today as a means of serving cake.

Through a confluence of technological innovation and sartorial shifts in the early 20th century, the handheld fan began to fall out of favor. The advent of the electric fan and air conditioning made it obsolete as a utilitarian tool, while people started holding cigarettes and other objects instead of fans. And with the streamlined silhouette that became popular through the Jazz Age, the ostentatious, bulkier baroque fans began disappearing in Europe and America. While still a part of Spanish culture in Andalusia's flamenco dance tradition, we have largely lost to history this once useful and beautiful object. *Set design & Photography by Charlotte Long*

On reading, fame and immigration.

MOLLY MANDELL

Junot Díaz

Earlier this year, Junot Díaz rescheduled a Los Angeles meet-and-greet in favor of lunch with an admirer. His fan? Barack Obama. Lunch? At the White House, during the final week of Obama's presidency. The reasons behind his invite echo, perhaps, those for which Díaz has also received awards that include the Pulitzer Prize for Fiction and a MacArthur Fellowship (also known as the "Genius Grant"). His novels, in the words of Obama, speak "to a very particular contemporary immigration experience," and are "steeped with this sense of being an outsider, longing to get in, not sure what you're giving up." Here, Díaz riffs on his own feelings of alienation and discusses how, following an upbringing during which he was seldom the center of attention, finding anonymity is akin to feeling "mission accomplished."

Why did you become a writer? I had a sense very early on that I wanted to be an artist, because I was taught that an artist inhabited a certain place in society that wasn't predicated on approval. To my young mind, an artist's practice had everything to do with exploration, experimentation and breaking silences. It seemed incredibly heady, very intellectual, and I was drawn to that deeply. I was this immigrant kid from a very poor and boringly troubled family who fell in love powerfully with books in ways that only the loneliness and the disorientation of immigration could explain. Reading was in some ways a compass and salvation. In that love I developed for books and reading, and in that curiosity and interest in this concept of the artist, I began to come together.

How does reading fit into your life now? Some hungers never dull. Everything for me seems to begin and end with books. I continue to read frantically. It's sort of like people who went hungry for a period in their lives. Their relationship with food is forever altered. They stock a refrigerator as if they were still going hungry. In the same way, I'm frantic about books in ways that I don't need to be. A friend of mine said to me, "I'm always looking for excuses to put myself in the way of really bad men" and I thought, "I understand that." It's not great for my writing, but people offer me opportunities to waste a lot of time reading, and I'm like, "Sign me up!"

How does the theme of immigration play into your writing? That might be the most autobiographical part of my work. For all my attempts to not fit in, I really do belong to my community. My books all have a central alter ego, Yunior, and he is simultaneously part of his community and in an enormous struggle with it. When I began to put that to language, as I was coming of age and in college, I realized what a wonderful curse that was for a literary character. What does it mean to be a member of the team and yet very critical of it? It's a way of permanently never being at home.

Where do you feel a sense of belonging? I often recreate and feel most at home with the community I grew up with—Dominican, African-American, working poor. Emigrating to the United States from the Dominican Republic added an extra level of consciousness, where there's always a distance between where I am and the island that I still call home. My little brother was born and raised in the United States and doesn't know anything about the Dominican Republic. He's not any less complicated than I. It's just that he only has one lens, though it's probably twice as thick as my two lenses. My identity is predicated on the idea that there are two worlds. When I'm in one world, I'm looking for the second.

Where else do you see the immigrant narrative depicted in popular culture? I'm always struck by how central an immigrant sensibility is to our modern experience. Even if we don't recognize it, the immigrant narrative is important for our way of understanding the world. Recently, I went to a meeting at an animation studio and they showed me their slate of films for the year. Every single film was about a character who is in one world and is either transported or travels to another world and is forced to learn its language. These films all tell immigrant narratives, but that's not something people want to be reminded of. It ruins the magic. Immigration is an idiom we speak very well but refuse to understand socially. We all can relate to these narratives in one way or another, so you would think it would draw us together more.

How do you deal with fame? I am very uncomfortable around the apparatus of being a "famous" writer, even though fame at the literary level trades at something like the Venezuelan bolívar. My dream in life is to disappear, to have anonymity. There are easier ways to get famous than what I've done. In spite of myself, I have received a certain level of attention. I think that everything I've done as an artist has been because I haven't been able to say what I need to say or get close to some of the things I've been through—the family traumas. It's hard to indulge fame when you grew up in a world of shame.

Tighten your belt to solve this trouser-themed puzzle.

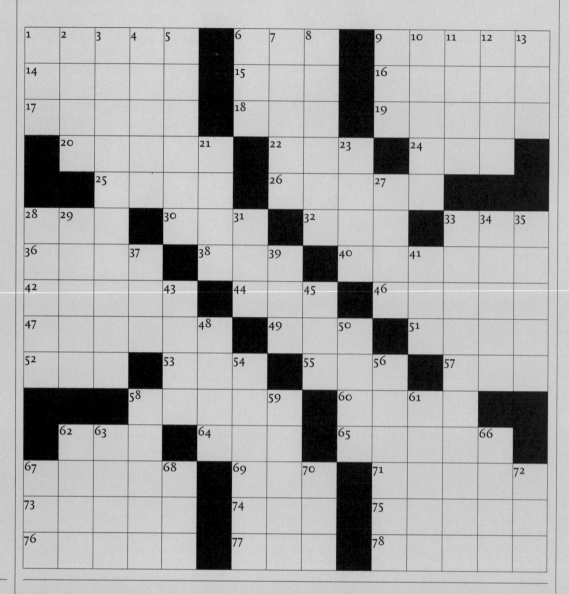

MOLLY YOUNG

Crossword

ACROSS

1. *Group in "Arabian Nights"
6. Core of a smartphone
9. *Racine or Rousseau, to name two
14. "La Bohème," or "Tosca"
15. Swiss mountain
16. "Take __ down memory lane"
17. Small plates, in Madrid
18. Tavern
19. Prone to complaining
20. Oxidizes
22. "Little Women" sister
24. Keats wrote one of these about a Grecian urn
25. Adolescent
26. The starred clues, in other words
28. Tax pro, in America
30. 1985 Akira Kurosawa film
32. Eastern philosophy
33. Loops in, for short
36. Loathe
38. Animal companion
40. Signature item for Fred Astaire
42. Sayonara in Spanish

44. Coffee alternative
46. French wine valley
47. Lickety-split, in Italian
49. Conclude
51. "Splendor in the Grass" screenwriter
52. Amartya who won a Nobel Prize in economics
53. Evergreen climbing plant
55. Homer Simpson catch phrase
57. Catch
58. Welcome
60. Beer ingredient
62. Murmur
64. Sunbeam
65. Digital communiqué
67. *Island in Campania region
69. Record number?
71. Backless heels
73. Picture
74. Prefix for some music and film genres
75. Panache
76. Like shoes
77. Paris-to-Bordeaux dir.
78. All set

DOWN

1. Spicy
2. On ___ with (equal to)
3. It may be tarnished
4. Delete
5. Guru
6. It can go on a pen or a head
7. Rubenesque
8. Cheerful
9. Prominent facial feature on a crocodile
10. Belief system
11. Dry as a desert
12. "A stitch in time saves ____"
13. John le Carré protagonist George Smiley, to name one
21. Lose one's cool
23. Tiny biting insect
27. Wrench, screwdriver, or hammer
28. *Fellas in Britain
29. "Father," en español
31. Fishing gear
33. Furry mammal that takes dust baths
34. *Classification for some ships and containers

35. Like some hills and bills
37. Lengthy stretch of time
39. Concert souvenir
41. Hawaiian taro porridge
43. Common cooking instruction
45. Also
48. Done with
50. Architectural feature of the Taj Mahal
54. Hankers
56. *Carpenter's item
58. Ravine
59. Taps a keyboard
61. Romesco or beurre blanc
62. Soldier's garb, for short
63. Luminous gemstone
66. Heavy metal used in bullets and batteries
67. "___ for Cookie" ("Sesame Street" song)
68. Roadside military danger: Abbr.
70. Trim the grass
72. Pigpen

Michael Anastassiades

Kinfolk's contributing editor *Michael Anastassiades* is a leading light on the global design scene. After a decade spent moonlighting as a yoga instructor, he leverages his personal quest for harmony and equilibrium into lighting design that features in the permanent collections of New York's Museum of Modern Art and London's Victoria and Albert Museum, among others.

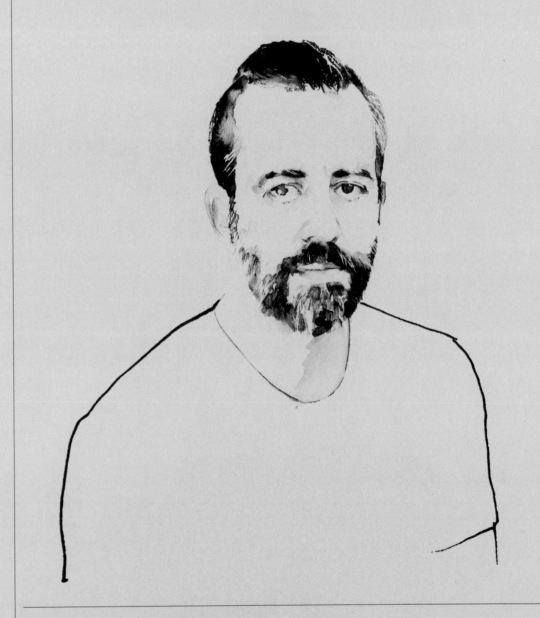

The first thing you do when you wake up: I write down my dreams
A prized possession: My collection of stones
The best advice you've ever received: A piece of yoga wisdom, "Practice and all is coming"
A place you'd like to visit: Greenland
A favorite museum: Archaeological Museum of Delos in Greece
A designer you admire: Thomas Edison
Your greatest fear: Mediocrity
The best light in your home: The evening light in my conservatory
A good habit of yours: My yoga practice
A bad habit: Missing it

Illustration: Chidy Wayne

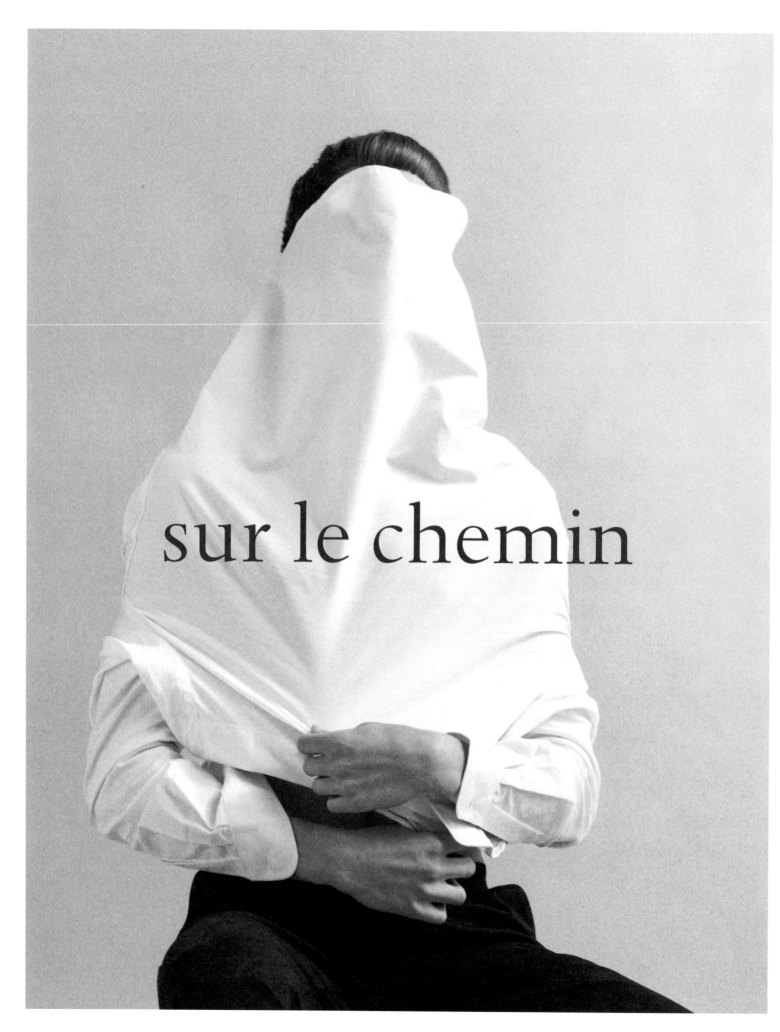

www.sur-le-chemin.com

Stockists

A DÉTACHER
adetacher.com

ANN DEMEULEMEESTER
anndemeulemeester.com

ANN-SOFIE BACK
annsofieback.com

BALLY
bally.com

BARBARA CASASOLA
barbaracasasola.com

BEAUFILLE
beaufille.com

BOMMA
bomma.cz

BOTTEGA VENETA
bottegaveneta.com

CALVIN KLEIN
calvinklein.com

CÉLINE
celine.com

CHLOÉ
chloe.com

CO
co-collections.com

COLOVOS
colovoscollection.com

COS
cosstores.com

CREATURES OF COMFORT
creaturesofcomfort.us

CTRLZAK
ctrlzak.com

DKNY
dkny.com

EDUN
edun.com

EMMA PAKE
emmapake.com

FEIT
feitdirect.com

FILIPPA K
filippa-k.com

HERMÈS
hermes.com

HUNZA G
hunzag.com

ICB
icbnyc.com

IITTALA
iittala.com

ISSEY MIYAKE
isseymiyake.com

JACQUEMUS
jacquemus.com

JENNI KAYNE
jennikayne.com

JIL SANDER
jilsander.com

JOSEPH
joseph-fashion.com

JW ANDERSON
j-w-anderson.com

LINDA FARROW
lindafarrow.com

LOEWE
loewe.com

LUISAVIAROMA
luisaviaroma.com

MANSUR GAVRIEL
mansurgavriel.com

MARGARET HOWELL
margarethowell.co.uk

MARNI
marni.com

MISSONI
missoni.com

M. MARTIN
mmartin.com

NATALIE WEINBERGER
natalie-w.com

NOVIS
novisnyc.com

PAUSTIAN
paustian.com

PRABAL GURUNG
prabalgurung.com

REJINA PYO
rejinapyo.com

ROSETTA GETTY
rosettagetty.com

SAMUJI
samuji.com

SEA
sea-ny.com

SOPHIE BILLE BRAHE
sophiebillebrahe.com

SONIA RYKIEL
soniarykiel.com

STELLA MCCARTNEY
stellamccartney.com

SUNAD
sunad.es

SUPERDUPER HATS
superduperhats.com

THE ROW
therow.com

TIBI
tibi.com

TOME
tomenyc.com

URIBE
studiouribe.co.uk

VITRA
vitra.com

WRKDEPT
wrkdept.com

YOHJI YAMAMOTO
yohjiyamamoto.co.jp

ZERO + MARIA CORNEJO
zeromariacornejo.com

Guiding you home.

From this classic Georgica Pond gem to contemporary
Sag Harbor retreats, discover the Hamptons' finest
real estate and the best agents to guide you there this summer.

compass.com

ISSUE 24

Credits

P. 29
Minotaure, Volume 8, with cover by Salvador Dalí, June 1936. Published by Albert Skira, The Menil Collection Library, Special Collections

P. 36 - 37
Artwork
Sol LeWitt (1928-2007),
Wall Drawing number #373: Lines in Four Directions (equal spacing on an unequal wall), 1983, Reinstalled in 2000, pencil, fixative, varnish, graphite, Indian ink and latex on wall, Gemeentemuseum Den Haag. Acquired from *Sol LeWitt* in 1983

P. 40 - 41
Production
Michelle Zollo

Photography Assistant
Jordan Strong

P. 50 - 61
Production
James Gear

Hair and Makeup
Caroline Gallyer

Casting
Sarah Bunter
Model
Imade at D1 Models

Photography Assistant
Ary van Giesen

P. 78
Photograph
Florette à la plage du Carlton, Cannes, 1956
Jacques Henri Lartigue
©Ministère de la Culture - France / AAJHL

P. 79
Photograph
Sylvana Empain. Juan-les-Pins, 1961.
Jacques Henri Lartigue
©Ministère de la Culture - France / AAJHL

P. 140 - 153
Production
Brooke McClelland

Models
Cheyenne and Ash at New York Models

Photography Assistant
Donna Viering

Styling Assistants
Julie Green
Barbara Ramos

P. 169
Flowers
Calla lily

P. 171
Flowers
Quince and heliconia

P. 172
Flowers
Anthurium

Vase
Natalie Weinberger

P. 173
Flowers and Produce
Musa, rutabaga, parsnip, artichokes and dragon fruit

P. 174 - 175
Flowers
Amaranthus, orchids

P. 176
Flowers
Cigar Lei by Cindy's Lei Shoppe in Honolulu

SPECIAL THANKS
Sam Adenborough
Pauline Cuchet
Elizabeth Ehrnst
Gemeentemuseum
Georgia O'Keeffe Museum
Kim Hoefnagels
Bonnie Nadell
Laura Thompson
Bo Thuesen